D1236291

Finding Higher Ground

ENVIRONMENTAL ARTS AND HUMANITIES SERIES

Finding Higher Ground

A LIFE OF TRAVELS

ESSAYS BY **CATHARINE SAVAGE BROSMAN**

UNIVERSITY OF NEVADA PRESS ▲▲ RENO & LAS VEGAS

Environmental Arts and Humanities Series

Series Editor: Scott Slovic

University of Nevada Press, Reno, Nevada 89557 USA

Copyright © 2003 by University of Nevada Press

Manufactured in the United States of America

Design by Carrie House

Library of Congress Cataloging-in-Publication Data

Brosman, Catharine Savage, 1934–

Finding higher ground : a life of travels /

essays by Catharine Savage Brosman.

p. cm. — (Environmental arts and humanities series)

ISBN 0-87417-538-0 (hardcover : alk. paper)

1. Southwest, New—Description and travel. 2. Texas,
West—Description and travel. 3. New Orleans (La.)—
Description and travel. 4. Europe—Description and
travel. 5. Identity (Psychology) 6. Place (Philosophy)
7. Regionalism. 8. Brosman, Catharine Savage, 1934—
Childhood and youth. 9. Brosman, Catharine Savage,
1934—Journeys. 10. Brosman, Catharine Savage, 1934—
Homes and haunts.

I. Title.   II. Series.

F787.B76 2003

917.904'33—dc21   2002012293

The paper used in this book meets the requirements of
American National Standard for Information Sciences—
Permanence of Paper for Printed Library Materials, ANSI
Z39.48-1984. Binding materials were selected for strength
and durability.

First Printing

12 11 10 09 08 07 06 05 04 03

5 4 3 2 1

For my daughter,

Katherine Brosman Deimling (Kate)

CONTENTS

Grateful acknowledgment is made to the editors of the periodicals where the following essays first appeared, occasionally in slightly different form: " . . . To Miss New Orleans," *Negative Capability* 13 (1993), edited by Dale Edmonds under the title *The Big Easy Crescent City That Care Forgot*; "The Immeasurable Sky," *Sewanee Review* 103 (Winter 1995); "Images of Paris," *Sewanee Review* 105 (Fall 1997); "Sneaker Ball," *Southwest Review* 84 (Spring 1999); "After the Flood," *American Scholar* 68 (Spring 1999), © Phi Beta Kappa Society; "Higher Ground," *Shenandoah* 49 (Summer 1999); "A British Interlude," *Louisiana Review* 1 (Summer 1999); "A House Apart," *Sewanee Review* 108 (Summer 2000); "Desert," *American Scholar* 70 (Spring 2001), © Phi Beta Kappa Society.

Finding Higher Ground

T his is a watershed book. My Louisiana friends, while concerned about flooding—as readers will discover—do not reflect much about watersheds (members of the Army Corps of Engineers, if I could count any among my acquaintances, would not fit this rule). Those residents of southeast Louisiana who are not water-control specialists or rural landowners and who do not travel widely and reflectively in other sections of the continent take for granted the dominant presence of the nearby Father of Waters and do not tend to visualize the sources and slopes that create it, since the area it drains is so large—most of the nation west of the Appalachians as far as the Continental Divide (with exceptions, especially the territory drained by other rivers emptying into the Gulf of Mexico or its bays: the Rio Grande, Nueces, Colorado of Texas, Brazos, Trinity, Sabine, Atchafalaya, Pearl, Alabama, Mobile).

In my Colorado girlhood, when we so often were more or less astraddle the backbone of the Rockies, we talked frequently about how, where, and for whom water runs. My father taught me thereby a great deal of geography and topography: how Redskin Creek runs into Buffalo Creek, thence into the North Fork of the South Platte River, which joins the North Platte to create the Platte, which courses then through Nebraska to its confluence with the Missouri, itself emptying into the Mississippi; and how Vasquez Creek is a tributary of the Fraser River, which joins and swells the there-modest but ultimately mighty Colorado River. (On some old U.S. Forest Service maps I have kept from my parents' collection, including one of the Arapaho National Forest drawn in 1932, I can trace all but the smallest of these local waterways.) Does my fascination with the liquid element, about which more is said later in this volume, spring from these early observations of trickles seeping from soil at high altitudes, rivulets racing, almost dancing, the nearly human force pulling them down the steep mountain slopes, and the understanding that the dividing line that makes some go one way, some another, is, even if irregular and difficult to discern at the highest point, absolute? Crossing one of the passes over the Divide meant sensing the pull of earth differently, crossing to another way of reaching the sea.

In our human stream, at most periods our lives just flow through undifferentiated and unremarkable territory, following the geographic lines and gravitational forces of our inner and outer existence—lines whose pull one feels, but generally as formalized or expressed by symbols, like traces on a map marking the Mississippi and its tributaries. But there are exceptional moments when we become aware of the terrain, or realize it has changed under us, and at crucial times we find ourselves on an apex, looking Janus-like at ourselves and our possibilities—the past sloping one way, the future another. In fact, of course, this is the phenomenon of every day, indeed, of every instant, but we cannot stop to reflect on it while we are finishing a report, driving on a crowded freeway, talking to a client, or preparing dinner—nor should we, I suppose, despite philosophers' admonitions to live each moment as if it were our last, as if our whole selves or a universal imperative were expressed thereby. Still, anytime when one can say, giving some meaning to the phrase, "This is the first day of the rest of your life," the moment constitutes a human watershed.

New Year's Day witnesses many such reflections, tiny illuminations complete with resolutions for change, but for most human beings in the Occident, as they pass from December into January, the dividing line is not sharp or deep enough to be very significant. Personal events such as graduation, marriage (or its dissolution), beginning a new career, a child's birth, a family death, a geographic move, illness overcome, a grave accident, deeply experienced love, conversion or another profound religious experience, or sometimes just a birthday to which special meaning is given, are more likely to bring genuinely new directions for the flow of our days. We mark these moments as significant on our mental calendars, sometimes in our diaries or in letters to friends, very frequently by public celebration or ceremony, so that witnesses can agree we have stepped onto different territory, with our loyalties, our resolve, our interests gravitating in a new way. Perhaps the arrival of the third millennium A.D. brought for some an especially strong sense of demarcation, not just a brief moment of frenzy and resolutions.

Some watersheds are more radical than others. Two days ago here in New Orleans, which has been for nearly thirty-five years my city of residence, a woman from Arizona, visiting some family members, tried to commit suicide by leaping from one of the parallel bridges I can see from my windows. Called, awkwardly, the Crescent City Connection, they span the Mississippi, joining the East Bank to Algiers, a district on the so-called West Bank (which is, in fact, more to the south and east at this point). The minister from Parker Memorial Methodist Church uptown happened to be passing by with his wife, en route home from a family visit. When his wife spied the woman at the railing and called out, "She's going to jump," he pulled over—in what was probably heavy traffic, with impatient drivers cursing behind him—opened his car door, and ran toward the railing. "Don't do it," he exclaimed. The frenzied woman answered that her life was "all messed up." (I don't doubt it.) "But life is too valuable to throw away; you can't just end it like this." He talked to her for several minutes—his clerical experience making the difference, perhaps—while his wife called the bridge police, who came in their vehicle, crept up behind, and grabbed the woman in a flash.

She had not come to New Orleans solely to jump, I suppose; something must have gone wrong during her visit here. She was to be taken for observation to the psychiatric ward of Charity Hospital. God knows what has become of her since; perhaps she will seek counsel from the good clergyman and comfort in his church, or return to Arizona with increased fortitude and a new understanding of her commitments and responsibilities, including those to herself. Having avoided a watery grave in the river, she may feel somehow renewed; I hope so. Bridges are favorite spots for those bent on ending their lives, but a bridge is also a means of spanning differences, or of crossing over to a new beginning. They also offer a vantage point on the otherwise undifferentiated Heraclitean flow of time and allow us to regain a sense of freedom from its passing. "That's water under the bridge," we say.

The watershed from and about which I write in these opening pages, by way of introduction to the essays that follow, is obviously not so radical: it is merely my retirement from professing language and literature, in one circumstance or another, for nearly forty years before groups of undergraduates and postgraduates and occasionally solo students. I hasten to add at once that this retirement was, in circumstances that the final essay explains, an early one, according to common measures. The thought is appalling that, without this bit of information, readers might visualize some senescent old crone, creaky-voiced, bent with age, or at the least rotting henceforth in inactivity—a frequent meaning assigned to the word *retirement;* neither my vanity nor my sense of how time should be used will countenance *that.* To be more precise, this retirement *was* early. But as the months, then the years, pass, my age and my status as retiree will cease to be out of harmony with each other. So, if I am to consider the meaning of this change in its original form, its original feeling—as a departure that is premature in one way but appropriate in another—I must do so *now,* from this watershed moment. The lines that follow pursue this topic. Readers will then find in the rest of the collection ruminations and accounts, not always following chronological order, from both sides of the divide, preretirement and postretirement, reaching back to my childhood in the form of memory, but dealing also with the present.

There may appear to be some contradiction here, or at least a metaphorical difficulty. Along a true watershed, the flow goes *down* both ways, finding small obstacles, doubtless, but pushing them out of the way or going around them, in what appears to be effortless movement, certainly unwilled, its power marked by its effects: worn riverbeds, rounded stones, boulders sent rolling, noisy cataracts. (As an Englishman remarked about Niagara Falls, "What's to stop it?") Occasionally these currents are dammed up, but—unless syphoned off for irrigation or forced by pipeline across a ridge— ultimately the streams make their way along the slope toward their confluence with other streams and finally the ocean. In the flow of our lives, in contrast, we struggle uphill a good deal of the time, like Sisyphus, forcing our burden and our character up inclines whose summits we do not see or see well, from which we may as likely as not roll down again (the struggle becoming failure or meaningless pursuit), or which, while rewarding to the climber, nevertheless turn out to be foothills to a higher challenge still. Thus do ends become means to new ends by the transformation of praxis.

In fact, this latter process is the most quintessentially human. Our ends are our meaning. Retirement—like graduation, a professional promotion, financial or other success, or, alas, marriage—sometimes encourages or at least allows people to "go downhill," so that the watershed metaphor fits well. Yet I have titled the closing essay of this collection "Higher Ground," suggesting that, even at a watershed time, our human direction must always be up, until utter decrepitude or death brings about that final decline and radical separation on the other side of which we cannot see. According to the song "Jacob's Ladder," which was current in my girlhood at camps and church events, and which as a student in Paris I heard sung movingly by a powerful American black man at L'Abbaye, a small Left Bank nightspot, "Every rung goes higher, higher . . . Soldiers of the cross." Whether seen in Christian terms or those of existentialism, or both, the human trajectory is by its very nature directed forward and upward, not toward decline. Decline is its ruin.

In my own experience, literal watersheds and higher ground are in fact very much connected, and for me the metaphors go together well, since in Colorado the Continental Divide as well as other minor and major watersheds (such as that between the Arkansas River and the Rio Grande, or the Gunnison and the San Juan) are generally at very high altitudes, along the precipitous ranges of the Rockies. The question arises whether going back to some of this territory, in fact and in prose (as readers will see), constitutes a return to a sort of Rousseauesque or Wordsworthian childhood innocence, that is to say, superiority: was that high ground of my young years truly a moral peak, from which the adult condition has inevitably separated me forever? I think not: I do not accept the views of these pre-Romantic and Romantic writers, or at least *my* view of their views. But, looking backward, as I shall in this volume, and retracing by wheel and language some of that girlhood territory, as well as other moments of the past and present, I do discern various sorts of elevation—as well as some unfortunate slippages—and perceive that *high* must be appropriate and proportional to the person, the age, the circumstances. So that my youthful experience *was* meaningful, with its own sort of excellence; and, if one cannot again regain elements of early authenticity or any prelapsarian truth that might have existed, one can perhaps find heights suitable to the new time, constituting, as one circles back, a spiral of understanding. Living appropriately ("vivre à propos")—that is the true masterpiece of man, wrote Montaigne.

When retirement appeared as a silhouette on the horizon, a dark rider coming toward me, or waiting as I rode toward him, well-meaning friends warned me of its dangers, having known others who, upon leaving the university and looking forward to their leisure, were miserable instead, finding nothing to do and no one to do it with. I assured them—without arrogance, I hope—that such would not be my case, enumerating my writing and research projects, travel plans, friends and family members, some elsewhere, whom I would visit, and trying to persuade them that, even without golf and gardening (neither of which I wish to take up), I would not find time weighing heavily on my hands. I had acquired, if you will, a large treasure on which to draw. Jean-Paul Sartre would call this "capitalization" and condemn it as a bourgeois impulse expressing not only a Calvinistic economy of acquisition and saving but also cultural retentiveness and class consolidation, therefore class oppression (of the proletariat). To consider, as he did (except, of course, when the subject was a fellow radical) as essentially corrupt, hypocritical, and of a piece with political or financial tyranny the commitments of mind and heart and the means by which they are promoted or the achievements and projects of the reflective or vital self—or the simple prudence of not spending everything one has—is absurd.

Sartre was not wrong, however, in perceiving that material possessions are, for many, a way of covering up their inadequacy and establishing self-identity, and that a job can serve the same purpose. Gisors, in André Malraux's *Man's Fate,* observes that "every old man is a confession," and that, if the old age of so many people appears empty, it is because they themselves were: their emptiness was disguised from others and themselves when they were younger and more engaged in the world. Perhaps they have lost their true selves: "One believes one possesses, and one is possessed," as André Gide makes a character remark in *The Immoralist.* Is this why some people, while able to do so, fear saying good-bye to their careers? I do not like to think of a profession, even of a more modest trade or other work by which one earns a living, as a Pascalian *divertissement,* a screen or diversion, which, albeit a livelihood, serves just as much to keep people from looking inside their vacuous selves or outward at the abyss. For those of us who have the luxury and the ability to transform work from a simple means-and-means relationship (one works to eat and pay rent and so forth, and eats and sleeps to work some more), activity, including remunerated employment, should carry a meaning that goes beyond itself—to new ends, I said, these ends being chosen in deep concordance with our true selves and our beliefs. Otherwise, why bother at all? Why not acknowledge life for the circular biological repetition that it then is and do as a sonnet by Christophe Plantin, a sixteenth-century French humanist and printer, seems to propose: "wait calmly at home to die"? If to "wait upon the Lord" and His dispensations is wise, that does not imply idleness or inertia.

This watershed from which I write now presents an opportunity for a long view backward at terrain traversed, transformed by the years that have flowed since then and the concurrent alterations in contour, lighting, and perspective. We are layered creatures, human archaeological sites, palimpsests—the old writing lying under the new, usually retrievable as part of our personal paleographic record, sometimes showing through to the present and creating with what we now are a strangely illuminating text or collage. I am not concerned here, however, solely with the past in its pastness. As I circle back in time, there is the knowledge that the West of my origins is also the mythical West of American imagination, as well as the direction in which the course of empire takes its way (according to Bishop Berkeley), where riding into the sunset means not a conclusion but a beginning. Thus I do not see this enterprise of mine as valedictory.

In the following essays, organized along narrative or thematic lines, I reconsider—sometimes in the context of automobile journeys and often as a sort of existential exploration—places where I have lived and associated experiences, often as aspects of the social and natural environment in which we all live. Particular attention is paid to arid lands and human connections with them. The state of Colorado figures prominently, in the form of old mental snapshots centered around my father's and mother's families and those images, much more recent, from pleasure jaunts made possible by my new mode of life. Texas, especially West Texas, is even more present, appearing at the outset as I recount a journey from New Orleans to Alpine in the Big Bend (where I went to high school, after my parents moved there in 1949 and where they lived until their deaths). The landscape and cultural features of Texas reappear later, with different emphases and locales, in the guise of another automobile trip, and turn up at the very end to introduce and conclude a long drive through and meditation on other parts of the West. There are also pieces set in France and England, where I have lived, and three essays connected in whole or in part to New Orleans, the city with one of the highest rainfalls and the lowest elevation in the United States, close to the mouth of the great river, truly at the bottom of the water system, if not its dregs. The genre of autobiographical writing, to which part of this very book belongs, concerns me in some of its specificity and fundamentals. Sentimental failures cannot but be acknowledged, even as I try to see relations with others in the most favorable light possible.

In moving over this territory, I deal, obliquely or directly, with some additional cultural, historical, social, and philosophic issues of our time and others, viewed broadly: the role of leisure; the place of the individual; women's identity; the meaning of community; relationships between person and place, nature and culture—thus what *home* means; use of resources; the interpretation and uses of the past; personal and collective ethics; ways of seeing ourselves in this universe. I have tried to offend no one whom I count among close associates; but *certain* judgments must be made, and some who appear here anonymously or pseudonymously—or who are well-known public figures—are depicted as they have appeared to me, their shortcomings undisguised. To my family members and friends on both sides of the Atlantic who made possible many of the experiences reflected here and have so often supported my work in various ways, in addition to enduring me and my idiosyncrasies, I am more indebted than they can know; they will forgive me, I trust, if I have inadvertently done them injustice. Similarly, to students whose minds very creatively intersected with mine, to those nameless figures who treated me with courtesy as I explored the little towns and roads of the mountain and desert West, visited Paris, and took up residency in the North of England, and, finally, to those who contribute to my life simply by sharing our New Orleans community, I am enormously grateful. May they understand so as they read the pages that follow.

The Immeasurable Sky

The crest of summer's wave comes early, arriving, in truth, while the calendar still says *spring*. Even if, meteorologically speaking, the character of the season is felt much more keenly during the canicular weeks of July and August, when night as well as day seems overcome with heat, unable to shake off its lethargy, the days of late May and early June are perhaps more essentially estival; they are the turning point, the fresh flower of the season. For millions of schoolchildren, students, and those older who, like me, have remained in the academy and thus live mostly by the calendar of youth, they offer a new self, freed from the garments of strict routine, having at one's disposal a prospect of time whose end one can pretend not to foresee and whose uses hold the promise of being as bright, as varied, as expansive as the summer itself.

So what shall I do with this precocious crest of summer? This time, it is going to carry me some 2,800 miles, across Louisiana and Texas, to New Mexico, and back. The trip will reacquaint me with space and sky in their western grandeur; it will also offer some cultural insights. With water bottle and sturdy Samsonite suitcase, I am in the car and, about fifteen blocks later, on the ramp to I-10 going west. (I also have a map, thoroughly out of date, a gift from the Gulf Oil Company back when service stations handed you maps for free; most of I-10 is not even marked. Why keep it, then? It is *historical;* besides, it has an excellent mileage table and the scale is large enough for these well-worn eyes.) With the great eye of day behind me in the eastern sky, still close to its resting spot and streaked with sleep, the morning is almost cool, so I roll down the window. Those who know the route between New Orleans and Baton Rouge, over the swamps and through the river parishes, will tell you that it puts one in mind of the Styx or perhaps, better, Lethe. It is appropriate that one of the waterways it crosses is called the Blind River. If you drive that way in rain, you risk losing your bearings. But this time the wind moving through the car creates freshness, the water of Lake Pontchartrain is silvered, the marshes are a golden green, and even the mournful cypress and Spanish moss, the choking water hyacinths, and the ghoulish dark pits of swamp water at the edge of the causeway are without eeriness.

Past Laplace, where the highway gets down from its stilts, I look out over the fields where cattle, as sleek and placid as those in paintings of the Dutch School, chew their cuds under milky lowland skies. Baton Rouge is up the road. Like the mad fifteen miles getting out of New Orleans and its fringes, the portion of I-10 going through the state capital seems to be a trial track for the upcoming Indianapolis 500; still, I manage to come out alive on the far side and cross the lofty bridge over the Mississippi, the great continental artery. Although little here resembles the West Texas and New Mexico landscapes toward which I am headed—and the cattle are actually *lying down,* whereas western ones, having only slim pickings, must graze continuously—in some senses I can say this is the *West,* so I may begin to feel at home. Furthermore, to judge by such superficial signs as cowboy boots, roll-your-owns, and weather-lined faces, many of the residents of South Louisiana have more in common with their western brethren than with those so much closer in New Orleans—a city that is sui generis anyway. (From my apartment windows in New Orleans, I can *see* the west side of the Mississippi; still, that is not the same thing as setting foot, or wheel, there, especially since, because of the crescent bend in the river, when I look toward the West Bank, over the bridges mentioned in my opening essay, I am really looking *east.*) Ahead now are the Atchafalaya Swamp and Lafayette—the heart of Acadiana—then the rice paddies of Crowley and Jennings, where, freed from the swamp forests, the horizon will open up. The air is warmer now, with a midmorning feeling; perhaps I should turn on the air conditioning. But in jeans and a work shirt, I still feel comfortable. Let's see: in the past, didn't we drive across Texas without cooled air—and with fewer fill-ups? As a challenge, I determine to try it again.

A stop for coffee at Landry's near Breaux Bridge is welcome; the dining room is dark and cool, away from the highway glare. Country music is playing at the back. As I stir and stir the nearly boiling brew, then take careful sips, two waitresses carry on about a bouquet of roses that has just arrived for a third; say what you will, the lover-boys in Cajun country know the ways of the world. The rattle of video-poker machines and one-armed bandits (installed when former governor Edwin Edwards and his cronies managed to bring what is called "gaming" to Louisiana, so that the poor folks who, unlike him, can't afford trips to Las Vegas can lose their money here) forms a bass to the waitresses' soprano chatter. (In obedience to the laws that protect the innocent, assuming there are any, the restaurant owners have dutifully strung a rope around the gambling area, in lieu of a partition, and added a sign, No Minors Allowed.)

Quite a while later, after a bite of lunch and across the Texas state line, past Orange and Beaumont, something seems to slap my rear fender. I slow down a bit. *Whap*—

another thud, then another. But no one is throwing cow pies at the interstate. Since stopping does not seem practical (the pastures on either side offer no oasis), I persevere. Finally, I reach a self-serve station and convenience store in Winnie. Well, not Winnie, exactly: greater Winnie. The town itself must be out of sight over the fields. The trouble, as anyone more knowledgeable would have guessed, is a tire: what remains of it, after what must have been rotten shreds flew off, is quite flat. Among my skills is not that of tire-changing. A teenaged cashier, just getting off her shift, offers to put on my spare ("mighty friendly," as the Texans say), but I have none, as it turns out. (I am driving a secondhand Chevrolet; the salesman had assured me that it had a full-sized spare under the trunk flooring. Should I have looked? Of course. So much the worse for me.) We call Winnie Tire Service.

While I wait, I inspect the signs around the cash register—signs that would bring grist to the mill of a sociologist, should any of that breed leave his urban territory and chance upon Winnie. The work ethic is well supported in mottoes and cartoons. There are also indications that the people hereabout think that, while the great wave of prosperity has passed them by, taxes have not, and I suspect that a number of Perot voters could be found in these parts. Here comes one of them now, perhaps—that is, if he went to the polls: the tire-service man, in a dented, mud-colored, and mud-bedecked Ford pickup. He is hirsute and unkempt, but has an amiable manner. It is evident that his lady friend beside him will shortly be involved in the sort of labor that only women can carry out, and she does not participate in putting on the new "tar"—contrary, I am told, to her custom.

On now to the cat's cradle of Houston freeways, which would give Daedalus a run for his money. One would not guess that it is well before the usual rush hour; why are these people not at the office? Or maybe

their vehicles *are* their office. Well, mine is a way of seeing—and I don't want to see this frenetic maze any
longer than necessary. I count on covering half the distance to San Antonio before stopping. Past six in the
afternoon, a little motel in Schulenburg, with a café
called the Old Smoke House, looks inviting. After a
shower, a meal of enchiladas (even in the part of Texas
settled by Germans you can get good Mexican food, and
I have been dreadfully deprived of all but the mild
Sonoran variety), and a postcard or so to my family, I
am ready to turn in.

The next day will offer a rich bill of visual fare, with
its vistas of range and sky. First, a fill-up (to be sure, the
drive without the air conditioner was a thrifty one), and
the purchase of a blue celluloid eyeshade that shows
two steers and says "Texas"—tacky, if you will, but utilitarian, since yesterday's glare will double once I reach
the desert. Then a hundred or so miles to San Antonio,
over increasingly deep rolls of countryside, although the
Hill Country proper is to the north and northwest. In
San Antonio, I leave I-10, which, as seekers of California
may recall, unless they consigned their trip through
Texas to the dustbins of their memory, goes up through
Boerne, Kerrville, Junction, Sonora, Ozona, Fort Stock-
ton, to Van Horn. Instead, I bear slightly southwest on
U.S. Highway 90, which will take me to Alpine for the
night. It is the longer route, but the familiar one, in-
scribed in my memory as well as in the desert. Despite
its desolate wastes, it is also dramatic, marked by curves,
canyons, mountains, and vast but varied prospects.

The first town west of San Antonio is Castroville, the
Little Alsace of Texas, looking indeed like some of the
villages between Strasbourg and Colmar. Pastry shops
are tempting, but I push on to Uvalde, once the home of
Vice President John Garner, where usually I like to stop
for lunch at the Holiday Inn (Mexican architecture,
mind you), because it serves outstanding enchiladas.
But the hour is still too early, so I order just a roll and

coffee, like the ranchers who gather there to chew the fat with their friends. With rare exceptions, I have seen the last of the cultivated fields today. Passing up the attractions of Brackettville, movie capital of Texas, with its ersatz Alamo and other scenery suitable for shooting westerns, I head to Del Rio and lunch. One hundred ninety-nine miles will remain this afternoon. The county is called Val Verde, but except for the banks of a stream in Del Rio, little green is visible, even on the shores of the Amistad Reservoir, where Mexico and the United States cooperated to dam up what is left of the Rio Grande after it has irrigated thirsty fields in New Mexico and downstream from El Paso. Beyond Del Rio are Comstock and Langtry, which appear in Larry McMurtry's novel *The Streets of Laredo*.

Before reaching Langtry, I cross the Pecos River, with its impressive black canyon and high bridge. This is the lawless territory over which Judge Roy Bean presided. The road also passes the Devil's River and the Dry Devil's River—not much of a distinction, since there is no water in either—and, after a while, I will drive by Hell's Half Acre. The terms are not misplaced. As the old joke has it, God gave the Devil the choice between hell and West Texas, and he took hell. For many miles there will be little but wilderness: Dryden, Emerson, and Longfellow—these names on the map, names in the mind of some literary-minded settler or railroad man, correspond to almost nothing on the earth itself. The air burns with a white heat, settled over dry sand and stones. But the sky is like a great living presence, with its mounds of white clouds, moving but pensive, its imponderable blue, and the wide embrace of its horizon.

After more than a hundred miles of territory barren of almost everything save creosote bush, a transformation becomes perceptible: by individual blades and sprigs scattered here and there, then multiplied a hundred, a thousand fold, the desert has turned green. Precipitation this spring must have been unusual. To the west of

Sanderson, a small railroad town by a dry gulch, even the cactuses are verdant. As the afternoon ripens, it grows dark; clouds fill the bowl of sky ahead of me, shaded from pearl gray to nearly black, and the air freshens. Lightning strikes its tinder over the far range, and thunder may be waiting in the wings. Might rain actually fall on me? I am reminded of the two ranchers who were looking up at the thunderous West Texas sky. One asked, "Do you reckon it could rain?" The other answered, "I hope so, for my son's sake. *I've seen rain.*"

Yes, indeed, rain will fall today—and abundantly. Not given to half measures, the Texas skies now pour out, in the place of inundating sunlight, a flood of water. The arroyos and "bar pits" ("borrow pits"—the ditches by the side of the highway) are running; patches of standing water from an earlier storm are visible across the sand. A deluge in the past that flooded half of Sanderson, others that washed out Alpine and carried away an earlier Pecos River bridge come to mind. During the last thirty miles of my drive, I might feel transported back to Louisiana—except that what little I can see of the landscape through the streaming glass hardly resembles the contours and flora of the lowlands.

With windshield blurred—maybe my wiper blades are as rotten as the old tire—I reach Alpine, along streets where water is running. Arriving at the house of my friends—friends, rather, of my long-deceased parents—I find Loyce sitting on the porch, awaiting me, but wrapped in a quilt, and Ralph (pronounced "Raf" in the Texas manner) inside because of the chill. We will have to eat supper inside. Radio station KVLF reports this rain as the biggest in years—over two and a half inches on the south side of town. Perhaps I should come more often.

Now, my ultimate aim on this trip, as I said, is to cross New Mexico from the southern border almost to the Colorado line, in order to visit my cousin Edith and her husband (who will reappear briefly later in this book), presently living in Taos. Having reached extreme West Texas, I am already close geographically and otherwise. But Alpine is not just a port of call en route, since to me it is, in some ways, *home*. Moreover, because I know it well, yet can take on it the perspective of a visitor, it is particularly suitable as a focus for some of my reflections. These last few years, we have been bombarded with talk about "diversity" and "multiculturalism." I daresay that the purveyors of such correct thinking would find West Texas "diverse"—at least if they could divest themselves of the rigidity that makes them acknowledge difference in only a few prescribed forms. They might have a hard time understanding the accent and quaint colloquialisms, some of which are holdovers from Scottish dialect, as in "redd up" (tidy up); they would wonder that anyone could find here the wherewithal to live, or to occupy his time; if honest, they would be obliged to admit that the inhabitants are probably deprived in some ways—*benighted* was formerly the term—and that no one is coming to rescue them. But the marginalized and disadvantaged (at least those officially acknowledged as such) have also, we are often told, rich realms of culture—fully as good as the dominant forms—to which we should all have access, supported by philanthropic and governmental agencies. So would the observers agree that there is any special cultural tradition to be found here? Or would the locals simply be dismissed as members of an undifferentiated majority, ignorant oppressors but oppressors nonetheless? Let's see.

One could approach the matter by detailing everyday features in Brewster County, such as the regional cooking (Mexican food, of course; barbecue—including *cabrito;* venison; pan-fried catfish from the Rio Grande; burgers-in-a-basket), the music (country-and-western plus Mexican popular songs of the day, sung in Spanish), the architecture (adobe, the hacienda influence, and Mexican ecclesiastical style), the outdoor life, whether for livelihood or recreation—ranching, hunting, rodeos (ah, but they attract much wrath). One could stress the co-presence now of two main ethnic groups and the rich historical background—Cabeza de Vaca and other explorers, the Spanish settlers, the Comanches, the garrisons to the north in Jeff Davis and Pecos Counties, mining, railroading—although those associated with this past, both English-speaking and Spanish-speaking, would generally be considered exploiters. (That *some* of their views and activities no longer meet with approval does not invalidate them *all*. The products of the past are synthetic, going beyond the wars and massacres that may have been a part of it.) In addition to the history and the local color, one could emphasize that many people living here have only the bare wherewithal for their needs; that should make them precious in the critics' sight. One could add that, among the older inhabitants, some escaped as wetbacks from unimaginable wretchedness on the other side of the border; others lived through the Dust Bowl years— and were dirt poor, so poor that, like people my mother knew in Wyoming, they had never seen two plates that matched. Some Texans of that generation rose out of it and were successful: Lyndon Johnson, born in the Hill Country, further east, is the supreme example. Others fared less well. Doesn't this background ratify their experience, Latinos and Anglos both, and identify them as a genuine cultural group?

Another matter concerns me, though, which goes beyond "culture" to what is now called "cultural studies" and their implications. The solitary drive in the clear air, surrounded by a vast arena for the play of thought, has led me to reflect on some of these matters. For my entire adult life, I have thought my concerns were cultural—the enjoyment of literature, music, and art, and the creation, study, and teaching of the former. Recently, I have discovered my error. "Culture" as defined by the new critics seems to consist chiefly in what is behind

and at the side of those products I took to be its manifes-
tations—not the book, for instance, but the mode of its
production; not the museums, but the economic and
social systems that made possible the assembling of large
collections and the construction of buildings to house
them. Now I do not deny that such issues have both
interest and importance, if we are to understand our
past, nor that their investigation has, legitimately, wid-
ened our appreciation of certain things. But after the
investigations, the creative work should survive, in its
irreducible singularity. I want to look at real eighteenth-
century still lifes; I want ultimately to enjoy the pages of
Rabelais and Montaigne, and the individual behind
them, not to struggle with a discourse on the construction of gender in the sixteenth century. If I liked Flaubert,
I should want to reread *Madame Bovary,* not neo-Marxist
analyses of hidden economic structures during the Second Empire or lucubrations about hysteria.

This hobbyhorse of mine does not quite fit the Texas
range, over which my eyes have been riding. Still, some
connection may perhaps arise. In its various forms, one
strain of culture has long been associated with the land:
pastoral poetry from the Greeks onward, English house
poetry, the Romantics' writings, and our own American
forms, from Walt Whitman to William Carlos Williams
and Robert Frost, not excluding southern and western
writers. I am not unaware how easily this tradition, despite its rural association, lends itself to attack as elitist—
for it is not revolutionary, not proletarian, and is produced mainly by an educated few; even Whitman and
Williams, as white men who could read and write, look
(to some) like oppressors, though the former is saved
partially by his sexual anomaly. The fact remains that
such poetry was, earlier, enjoyed by thousands—many
more than enjoy any poetry now, probably; the French
Romantic poet Alphonse de Lamartine could say to a
detractor that his book would soon be in every cobbler's

pocket. Many American rustics were readers. A painting reproduced in *Scribner's Magazine* for January 1909 shows a sheepherder at night by his fire, with shapeless old headgear, rough clothes and boots, and a *book*. A sheepman from Ozona, Robert Maudslay, recorded in his diary the contents of the library in the two-room stone house he shared with his brother before the sheep market collapsed under Grover Cleveland: a complete Shakespeare, a complete Scott, the *Illustrated London News* going back to 1840, and sundry other volumes. Moreover, the great democratic broadening that American culture has witnessed, although tied partly to industrial urbanization, was also a function of the pastoral tradition, in which the individual sensibility, in a relationship to nature and society alike, was the touchstone.

What seems overlooked by the cultural critics is this connection of human beings to the land. I am not familiar with the personal views on such matters of one of their high priests, Michel Foucault; perhaps he resembled Sartre, who, although Simone de Beauvoir did manage to drag him along sometimes on excursions in the countryside, professed repeatedly his dislike of nature, to the degree that he tolerated fruits and vegetables only when cooked. Certainly I have not seen evidence in Foucault's writings, nor in those of another guru, Walter Benjamin, nor in those of their sometime-bedfellows the deconstructionists, of the literary tradition I have in mind. They have even less use for belief in the organic and moral connection between all life and the spirit (call it what you will). For them, the individual himself counts for little—only collectivities matter—so the subjective experience of a response to nature cannot amount to much.

I do not mean to imply that those are unfulfilled who have not driven Highway 90 across West Texas or some similar route, nor that, had they done so, the cultural critics would have reached different conclusions. What

I do mean is that the latter's understanding, for various reasons, is gravely flawed. It may be objected that they come out of a totally different intellectual context—Marxism, anarchism, structuralism, deconstruction. Indeed. Then why in the Sam Hill have they come *outre-Atlantique* to push it onto us? (Or, since I think the main reason can be divined, why have we been such dupes as to welcome them?) Recently I attended a conference at which three black-shirted, black-trousered, black-cravated French expatriate intellectuals, all remunerated generously by the state university system of California, held forth for our benefit on the evils—not just inadequacies—of the American liberal arts curriculum and the necessity of replacing it with "interdisciplinary" studies emphasizing the construction of race, class, and gender and the institutionalization of oppression. Having observed around them doubtless considerable progress in the replacement of the literary canon by nonmainstream works, and of Western history by studies organized around "groups," they seemed particularly anxious to take on the exact sciences; could it be that the type of careful reasoning that comes into play there is felt as threatening, or do they blame the scientists, who come out of the modern analytic tradition, for all social ills?

They would feel little but scorn for the people here in West Texas, where the individual has counted for so much, who still hold to the validity of personal experience and feel kinship with the land around them, and for most of whom the heavens are not empty, since a benevolent Deity still has his place there. Such faith, unfathomable and immeasurable, is that personal truth of which Søren Kierkegaard spoke, held fast in one's subjectivity and beyond demonstration. Whereas the nineteenth-century scientific spirit denied the validity of such experience in the name of the evidence of the external world—there was no scientific proof of the intervention of God in human affairs, or of the existence of a divinity anywhere, while evidence *did* exist that creation had not come about as holy writ had it, said writ thus being completely undermined—the new naysayers object on different grounds, namely, that such concepts as the self and knowledge are fraudulent constructions of oppressive Occidental institutions, perpetrated through the dangerous individualism of the Enlightenment and by means of a solipsistic, nonreferential language that ultimately says and knows nothing, but serves thereby as an instrument of oppression. Relativism has done in the very mind that identified it. According to these voices, moreover, all is really a function of collectivities, which behave according to their own dynamics, misunderstood by traditional historians. There is no author, hence no authority. ("Question Authority," says a bumper sticker. Well, I question that of the sticker.) If the self is unreliable—an illusion—so is experience: how can there be an action without an agent? And faith, hope, love, delight, sorrow—not to mention literature—these *are* actions, requiring self-awareness and identity.

Around the kitchen table—no need to use the dining room, since here I am considered as family—we eat the delicious tamales and enchiladas that Loyce has prepared. By supper's end, the celestial comedians have finished their declamations; *exeunt* all, except a few clouds, mopping up. We look out at pale streaks of blue vaguely edged by yellow, shading off to vermilion where, like an afterthought, the sun shows through before it cracks on the jagged hills to the west. A blanket will be necessary tonight, and tomorrow, heading northwest, I will have a cool start before I hit the lower elevations near El Paso. On every side, the Chihuahuan Desert will unfold its inexhaustible otherness, which mediates my own, as the range of the mind is relieved of its humours, its haze, and the circumscribed horizon of routine. The black-shirted intellectuals will be far away. Doubtless some lines of familiar pastoral verse will come to mind when I pass sheep grazing among the stones; or I can whistle a few bars of Beethoven's Sixth. Perhaps, even, steely clouds will pile up again, as the immeasurable skies display their evidences, for the greater delectation of the earth.

A House Apart

When I refer here to the number 1101, what I have in mind is not a date—some event in post-Hastings England under Henry I, for instance, or that of a (hypothetical) newly discovered manuscript of the *Chanson de Roland* antedating by thirty years what is now viewed as the oldest—but an address, that of my grandparents in Denver for about the first eight years of my life as well as for decades of their lives before that. This house, at 1101 East Alameda Avenue, was on streetcar line number 5, at the corner of Corona Street, just a block from the commercial corner of Downing Street, which had two pharmacies, a Continental Oil filling station, Milliken's Market, and, next to it, a small dry-goods store, at which, I was told, my grandmother, who reared six children, bought socks every Saturday when they were young. Steele School was not much farther away, and then, within a half-mile or so on Vine Street, my uncle Kenneth's house and, a bit farther, our own. A mile or so in the same direction was the Denver Country Club, at which my father caddied as a youth: golf carts had not yet been invented, nor had health clubs proliferated.

My father had been born at that address and, except for a short time at Northwestern University in Evanston, Illinois, had lived there continuously until his marriage.

He had taken streetcar number 8, which also ran on Alameda a bit farther down the hill, to classes and his fraternity house at the University of Denver. It had also been home to his older brothers until their marriages or departures for medical school or elsewhere, and was still home, most years, to his two sisters: no one left home except to marry or go to another city. To him, it was the *locus amoenus,* the center from which one turned toward the rest of life, the measure of things; its affective power surpassed that of any words. Yet in my memory, my father never referred to it other than as 1101, the number—to him—standing synecdochically for the house. Precisely what the house itself stood for I can never know, but I imagine a complex, both factual and mental, of his parents (whom I remember well, for they lived to be very old); his brothers and sisters; all older; next-door friends (one Albert King in particular); and the fundamental affective experiences of a child, then a boy, a college man, finally, alas, an adult. Even if he did not agree with it entirely, he surely would have understood, as do I, Leonard Woolf's statement in *Beginning Again:* "In my experience what cuts the deepest channels in our lives are the different houses in which we live—deeper even than 'marriage and death and division,' so that perhaps the chapters of one's autobiography should be determined by the different periods in which one has lived in different houses."

The house at 1101 was a red-brick Victorian edifice, with a large front porch, the trim forest-green and white, the number painted in large gold figures on the transom, and an iron fence around the property. As a small child, my father was told by someone, in the depths of winter, to put his tongue on the frozen railing; some membrane stayed. This house and address were eventually replaced by others: in the 1940s, some years after my grandfather retired, my aunt Flora persuaded the family to move to a more fashionable and less commercial area, at Seventh Avenue and Josephine, which looked onto a broad parkway and where the facilities in the kitchen and bathrooms were much more modern. The habit continuing, it was known as 2410. (When, later, we lived in Texas, my father would say, coming back from the post office, "There's a letter from 2410," or ask, "Are you going to write to 2410 this week?") My grandmother's mountain cabin, near Bailey, on the way to Kenosha Pass, was the rustic extension of the two addresses; weeks spent there in the summer were certainly among the most pleasant of my memory. Still later, after both her parents were dead, Aunt Flora purchased a house on Jersey Street, known to all of us as 345. Though she appreciated the large, sloping garden and had a handsome sunroom added to what was already an attractive colonial design, we all agreed that it did not have the character of the previous residences. After everyone else in their generation was dead, she and Aunt Mary bought from my uncle's heirs, who all lived elsewhere, his Vine Street house, thus keeping it in the family; I sometimes thought of it by its address of 335, but to whom would I have called it that when I lived more than a thousand miles away? In her later years, when I visited in Denver, Aunt Flora and I occasionally drove by 1101; it hurt her to see that the neighborhood had declined and the house had taken on a shabby appearance. She had fantasies of buying it again to restore its proper character—knowing full well in her heart that neither the past of the house, nor her own, could be recovered.

All these houses had two storeys, plus a spacious basement. At one time, it was not thought suitable to have bedrooms on the ground floor, and by the time that mode of thought had changed, with the building of so-called ranch-style houses, some still kept to custom, or believed it safer to sleep one storey above the street. The house at 1101 had, in addition, an attic, to which one gained access by a narrow staircase leading from the upstairs sitting room. The attic must have served as a children's bedroom in one period. By the time I can re-member, it was the domain of two people only: Grand-father, who had his typewriter there on an olive-green table in the front half, as well as many books and file folders, and Aunt Mary, who, when home in the sum-mers and at Christmas from her teaching jobs in various Colorado towns, used the back part as her bedroom. It contained a brass bed and a marble washstand, with a china basin and pitcher. I considered it a privilege to be allowed to ascend the stairs, look around, perhaps touch the typewriter. There were also a glassed-in back porch at ground level, a screened one on the second storey, a small cantilevered sunroom—again, my grandfather's domain—and the basement, painted mostly dark green, which contained mysterious storage areas, some with Grandfather's chemicals, and a large boiler almost fright-ening in its fiery noises. A garage, which had served as a stable in the early years of the twentieth century, after Grandfather purchased the house, had been converted for motorcars.

When my father was a boy, what activity there must have been, children racing up and down stairs (a back set as well as the front staircase doubled the opportu-nity), in and out, down the street. (Not in the parlor, however: for his generation, as for mine, it was, except for certain purposes or on special occasions, off limits, enclosed by double doors and heavy horsehair curtains.) The boys did not always obey decorum or the rules. They kept animals upstairs on occasion, doubtless to Grandmother's displeasure; I recall hearing how once a pet squirrel fell through an opening in the bathroom floor (intended to let in heat from the kitchen below) onto the hot stove. Often my aunt Flora, sick abed for some seven years with rheumatic fever and its complica-tions, could not join in the activity. Perhaps that ex-plains why, in her seventies, she was still like a child, an unfulfilled creature of play who first had rested, when a child does not want rest, and then had worked all her adult life; quick to embrace any delightful prospect, she feasted on amusement, travel, and friends, and she was a perfect companion to a band of children on the lawn.

The lineaments of 1101 are so deeply graven into my neurons that, when I read novels whose domestic settings bear even a remote resemblance to it, I visualize the episodes as taking place in *its* parlor, in *its* back garden, at *its* front door. Cooks stoking an iron range or rolling dough for scones, or washerwomen leaning over large copper boilers, are in my *grandmother's* kitchen or at the gas stove on the back porch, used for heating the boiler and for summer cooking. Most fictional Christmas dinners, of course, take place in the double parlors of 1101, the doors thrown open. (Do I taste now the plum pudding and hard sauce, or is it my imagination?) The scene of partings, from which there may be no return, is the front hallway, where in fact my uncle Jack said good-bye for the last time to his parents, brothers, and sisters when he left in 1942 to go to the Pacific on a destroyer. The famous Proustian staircase from *Swann's Way*, which the narrator must ascend against his will, sent to bed early by a thoughtless grandfather, and whose smell of varnish, penetrating his being, gives a sharp physical form to the deep neurotic anxiety he feels at being separated from his mother without his good-night kiss, or viaticum (in Latin, a purse given to a traveler in preparation for a journey), is really the front staircase at 1101, in dark varnished oak, with heavy carpet and a stained-glass window at the landing, a large clock at the top step, and the lonely darkness of separation everywhere above.

I, fortunately, was not unhappy in that setting; whatever anxieties arose in my childhood—and there were many—were not associated with 1101. If grandparents are, as today's wisdom has it, much happier in that role than earlier as parents, because they can have the enjoyment and pride without the discipline and responsibility, grandchildren likewise can find the relationship rewarding. Not that my grandparents would not have disciplined me—I am sure they did, and their word was law—but the daily task of rearing the child was left to the generation in between, the one without prestige because it is so close at hand. Wonderful auras inhered at 1101, and the nearly white hair and wrinkles on the old people there, joined to the wit and ebullience of always-young maiden aunts, must have added to the charm everything had for me. There were, first, the grand piano and organ in the parlor; my first keyboard lessons took place at that piano, and, as a treat, Aunt Flora would sometimes allow me to play a bit on the organ keyboard (the pedals being out of reach). There were books everywhere, mostly well beyond my ken but creating a library sense in almost every room. Lovely art objects brought back from various travels added their exotic appeal. In the kitchen, beside the iron range, was a wing chair in green wicker, with cushions, whose arm rests disguised deep bins that contained magazines and other entertainments. A chow dog named Chang, my grandmother's, was part of the scene, but I had been told not to pet him, for he did not like children's attention. In the bathrooms and at the washbasins in each bedroom there was Pear's soap, its aroma bespeaking cleanliness. Often there was whistling in the house, as someone went about the day's work with a cheery note, and I can hear still my grandmother's voice, with her charming Scots-Irish accent, calling up the back stairs, "Flo-o-orrra." The afternoons always afforded time for tea—and sweets—either in the kitchen or dining room, but for me it was juice, not a caffeine drink—often grapefruit juice with Ritz crackers. And there was the sofa bed in the upstairs sitting room, on which I slept on overnight visits; the light from the streetlamps filtered in a bit through the curtains in a friendly fashion, and the streetcars' bells and trombone crescendo, all through the evenings, enhanced the pull of sleep. Then there could be splendid games of hide-and-seek, involving my cousins from Vine Street or, sometimes, Aunt Flora herself.

Perhaps there was something more, a kind of autonomy of spirit. *Sufficient unto itself* is the description I would engrave on the front pediment. Not that one can live without ties to the world, economic and material ones at least. But there were an independence of mind and conduct and a sense of authenticity in that family that served them well. They did not follow others' uses; they set their own. My grandmother was probably most responsible for this. Foolish though it might appear, her sense, after decades of living in the United States, that she still belonged to her native Canada made her resist, or was a sign that she would resist, pressures to conform—in speech, in dress, in habits. Gentry, and prosperous gentry, she and Grandfather remained completely aloof from society, such as it was in that young, brash western city; they attended concerts and lectures and so forth but not to be *seen*. Their daughters-in-law found, upon marrying, a tightly knit and idiosyncratic family fabric into which they were obliged to fit as well as possible, and adjustment must have been difficult sometimes. The individual strength—which was, ultimately, a moral one—that developed from such a family-grounded, inward-centered experience was not inconsiderable; in my father's generation, there is much evidence of it. Perhaps I learned it there, too. Certainly, as a child I cared almost nothing for what anyone thought except the family. Inconsiderate, even monstrously unheeding as this attitude appears—and I am sure it caused worry to my parents, who were finely attuned to people's needs and feelings and wanted me to learn to make accommodation for and with others—it preserved me from much adolescent unhappiness and, in a more civil, less abrasive form, has served me well in the rest of my life.

There reigned also in that little world the conviction that women were the peers, not the inferiors, of men.

Or so it seems to me now. At any rate, the aunts, like my grandmother, attended college; they later pursued different sorts of postgraduate studies in other states and abroad, worked, bought automobiles, traveled. (Meanwhile, on my mother's side, I had not only her example and that of my aunt Margaret, established in their respective professions, but also the models of Frances and Elizabeth, cousins much older than I, who got college degrees, had careers as well as families, and proved themselves in innumerable ways.) While the family structure at 1101 was a traditional one, the women tending to the kitchen and so forth, the division of labor did not appear to imply inequality of persons. I believe— I hope—that these women felt themselves most of the time as absolute, not relative.

It takes, to be sure, recognition on both sides for this to be so: no matter what her inner convictions, a woman whose worth as person is not acknowledged implicitly by men because they are stupid or brutish will have moments of inward rage, or find it necessary sometimes to assert herself pointedly. Strident voices are heard everywhere on that topic today; perhaps my own seems a bit harsh on this page when I observe that today's radical, and wholly unreasonable, feminists, as patronizing as those they attack, either believe or feign to believe that no one discovered autonomy before them. There is, they should learn, more than one way of feeling oneself as an absolute. Current policies that single out women for favor in any sort of competition, including professional and business spheres, aggravate the problem, leading those affected and those at the sidelines to suppose that only what amounts to paternalistic protectionism (how they would dislike the term!) and handicapping, as in golf, will allow women to achieve anything.

Yet I do acknowledge that my aunts on occasion encountered condescension and ignorant dismissal of them as competent and independent agents. Aunt Flora's diminutive stature added to that; she would go into a rage over those who, physically as well as figuratively, pushed her out of the way, as if she did not count. I suppose their attitude should be baptized *sizism*. I should add that, whether in a religious or political framework, a proper understanding of our fellow human beings, or simply common courtesy taught at home, should render official campaigns against such an *ism* and others unnecessary. Good heavens, do we have to have enforced sensitivity-training seminars paid for at a cost of tens of millions just to know that one should not despise or neglect a person on account of skin color, age, sex, and so on? Sunday schools used to teach that, I thought— and they were much less expensive.

Aunt Flora's size must explain why she was fond of large and powerful automobiles and liked to display their horsepower on mountain roads. This leads to an anecdote. One year in the 1970s, she went to a Buick dealership in Denver to buy herself a new car. Faced with a woman of small stature who was dressed in practical garb that apparently gave no impression of means, a salesman was patronizing to her; there was some suggestion (which I suppose no one would make now, because one really doesn't need to have much in the bank to sign up for any purchase) that perhaps she did not have enough money for a model in which she showed interest. She had, at the time, the wherewithal for it in her purse—several thousand dollars in greenbacks, I mean. She walked out, went to another dealership not far away, and bought a large wine-red Dodge. Aren't we warned to be ready for angels coming upon us unawares? In that case, as in so many, it was not true ill will on the salesman's part—after all, gain knows no prejudice—but stupidity.

Although he and I shared 1101 as a childhood place, the house for me was not, to be sure, quite the house my father had known, because then *he*, not I, was a child, and his parents, though middle-aged by the time of his birth, could not be grandparents to him (and he had none, although an old aunt remained). What was it like to grow up there in the first quarter of the twentieth century? When he was born, Queen Victoria had been dead only a few years; the Boer War was recent; a greater war would begin when he was seven and two elder brothers would put on the khaki. Having been born during the Civil War (or, as Grandmother, a Southern sympathizer, always called it, the War Between the States), his parents were really of the nineteenth century, but they adjusted well to the enormous changes that they lived through in the first half of the next one. Some of his boyhood books that remain in my library, after all these decades and countless moves, tell what he was thinking about sometimes. He owned a small illustrated Robin Hood; a large volume with plates called *The Boy's King Arthur;* a delightful book for the young reader entitled *The Blowing Away of Mr. Bushytail,* which included a character named the Ring-Tailed Snorter; *Tales from Washington Irving's Traveller;* and other gems, either classics for boys or whimsical products of the period. To these, in my library, I add his college books, such as Trevelyan's *History of England* and many of the great British writers.

He traveled, too, as a boy, going to Montreal and the surrounding area with Grandmother and one or more of his sisters and brothers. And he engaged in some sports (tennis and baseball, I think), went to camp in the mountains, following his brothers, and later worked in the summers at Estes Park. When, as I remember it, he would speak of his camping years and then the working summers in the mountains, it was in a tone that I recognize now as one of powerful nostalgia: a boy thinks long, long thoughts, and the leisure of the summer, the friendship with others, the physical activity in the high elevations, the natural beauty, and the vital drive that is the property of youth had led to an affective experience that few adult moments, I fear, could rival.

There is, however, no life, not even a young one, without friction, without resentment and disappointment. Did he, as I, wish sometimes he had never been born? Probably so; it is common, if not universal. It happened to me at age ten, as well as earlier; not long afterward, I think, I made my pact with life, and, through later unhappiness worse than anything the child could have known, because utterly without remedy, the pact remained: "Live, whether it be in distress or gladness." The demons do not go away, but if one is fortunate, they gradually change back into daemons, our inner divinities or guardian spirits. I have written elsewhere of Father's difficulties in business as a young man and then his erratic teaching career. There must have been friction sometimes at 1101 stemming from his uncertain professional life. Moreover, although he was a remarkably peaceable man as an adult, surely there must have been rows during his childhood. He certainly witnessed some: his sisters often quarreled—rivals, probably, for their mother's affection. Mary, the elder, established strong ties with her mother (they had a joint bank account and often traveled together), but Flora, the younger, was favored in some ways because of her illness. Although I was always utterly devoted to them, I recognize that each could be unreasonable with the other, and that this unreasonableness persisted till the end, through the years when, both retired and having no one else to live with, they lived together. A peacemaker like my father, I often tried to smooth over things, but when one was cross with the other and wanted to make it clear, there was little I could do. (The autumn before Aunt Flora died, she made a point of telling me how cruel her sister had been toward her during her childhood, saying "I want you to know"; more than her increasing fragility, this suggested to me that she was preparing to meet her Maker, perhaps bringing herself to forgive her sister in her heart but wishing, nonetheless, for some sort of testimony to remain. That, as an adolescent, Mary had long been burdened with part of the care of her sick sibling may shed light on the matter.)

I think my father was temperamentally ill suited to engage in such quarrels, even to witness them. He did not imagine harmony where it was not, but at least he was harmonious himself and held his tongue wonderfully; only once did I see him lose his temper. What price does one pay for such self-control and equanimity; what price does one pay for acting on oneself rather than the world, as Descartes urged? Sometimes I think that such serenity, achieved through inner discipline, is unnatural and unhealthy: why not explode, as others do, and simply tell people what fools or scoundrels they are?

Recently I was called to the office of a university official, apropos of some disagreement. She cited a dozen reasons to explain her position, some of them patently untrue (and a dozen reasons are never as good as *one*, anyhow), trying to disguise her prevarication with an unctuous, patronizing, and hypocritical cordiality. A French friend cannot believe that I didn't discharge a few verbal cannonballs or poison darts. More's the pity: I suffer from self-control and adherence to convention, which says one does not lose one's temper. So afterward, my unfortunate friends have to listen to the narrative of the interview and what I thought but did not say. But civility is what makes life possible: the woman's oleaginous hypocrisy was, I realize, necessary to *her*, to allow her to manage an unpleasant situation forced upon her by circumstances and a superior who didn't want to deal with it himself.

With an exquisite civility himself, Father was still not happy in a world where manners covered greed and exploitation and unkindness more often than not, and it took its toll: he was not a well man. Certainly his lack of worldly success sprang not from incompetence in the normal sense but from the need for tranquillity around him as well as within—for harmony between man and action, individual and others. He did not get this a great deal, and so sought refuge in pastoral reveries—sometimes the real desert setting of biblical seers—and other types of escapism, including literature, of course, and leaving jobs or simply not working at all. Unwise according to the world, it was his accommodation between fact and desire. Voltaire's story "Memnon, or Human Wisdom" begins thus: "Memnon one day conceived the insane plan of being perfectly wise. There is scarcely a man to whom this folly has not sometimes occurred." I conclude, looking at my own failures, that it is imprudent always to be prudent, unwise to pretend to much wisdom, and, short of a Trappist retreat, impossible to escape from the world.

What thoughts have come now from that house of my memory, like the variegated needlepoint thread in my grandmother's workbasket and the colored yarns with which she knitted her afghans, or the stained-glass panels in the landing window at 1101, or the various ways in which her six children, and then her grandchildren, devised ways of growing, being, loving, acting, dying! The reader will see that, leaving some of these threads loose, I have followed and woven together others, the house always at the center as a narrative theme and controlling image. Like so many other human ways that are rooted in nature, is our connection to a house powerful through an ancient animal need for the protection of den, nest, or cave and its nurturing reproductive group? Is it yearning for a closer nestling yet, that of egg or womb? Is it, in contrast, an expression of the impulse of *homo faber* to exteriorize himself by projecting outward his inner lines and spaces in deeds and works, whether verbal, musical, graphic, or architectural—the latter being a three-dimensional rendering of the dark cave of the mind and its mnemonic cabinets? *House* in English versions of Greek tragedy and the Bible and countless occurrences thereafter means *family group, lineage, legitimacy,* sometimes *right* (or *privilege*); it is close to the founding principles of society as well as the basic biological urge to mate with the best specimens. That it seems written into our blood—another metaphor for house and lineage, of course, as well as a physical fact—seems, then, like a work of our deep nature.

As I compose this essay, my cousin Beth, Frances's daughter, who is my age, has called from Colorado Springs to say that her mother, who has been ill for some time, is not expected to recover. (I shall visit her once more, however, as the last essay in this volume tells.) Reminiscences richly cluster around the thought of her, including houses in Woodland Park, Manitou Springs, and Cheyenne Mountain, all near Colorado Springs, where I stayed with that branch of my family as a child, and the house in the New Mexico desert where, much later, she and her husband, J. C., invited me to visit. That such images of the past are going through her own mind now—in the midst of what computer people call system failure or crash, and nuclear engineers call meltdown—but with pain, barely assuaged by morphine, I cannot doubt. Beth reports that Frances said the other day, when asked how she felt, "Better. Dad has just put a pot of coffee on the stove." Having withdrawn from life's continuation, for which she is no longer fit, and blocking out the claustrophobic isolation cubicle in which she has been pierced by needles and tubes, with her hands tied down(!), she is able to go back and inhabit the places of the past, feeling the cold winter mornings at the Woodland Park ranger station when she had to dress quickly in a chilly room and get a breakfast of her father's flapjacks and coffee before she drove down the road in the snow to preside at the schoolhouse, or seeing a flashing memory of the day's end, after labor all around, when she poured herself another cup, went to the porch, and gazed out at Colorado's most celebrated peak in repose across the valley.

Unlike the snail, we cannot carry around on our bodies a house with which we have an organic bond; instead, we carry it inside. Times and time have separated me greatly from the places and people and ways that

1101 evokes. Surrounded though I am by handsome nineteenth-century houses in the Garden District of New Orleans, I nonetheless own an apartment in a high-rise building dating from the 1960s, and before that I lived in a house from the same period. I suppose I could have attempted to marry some scion of one of these propertied families and thus gained admittance to a grand estate behind the fences and hedges, but, as Gide wrote, "It is folly to envy others' happiness; one wouldn't know what to do with it." The architectural delights are here for all to observe (and they contribute to the cityscape that will be part of my daughter's inheritance from her birthplace). The affective ones are in my heart.

In fantasy, which is surely one of the reliefs of the mind, I can return to 1101, hear my grandparents' voices, imagine a young man there, or stand at the piano with Aunt Mary playing and all of us singing Irish songs or Christmas carols—and later, fate having served me in this circumstance as in many, go to sleep to the sound of streetcars at night, this time not wheezing up the Denver hill but crescendoing along St. Charles Avenue, stopping, starting again, their bells clanging above the flow of pleasure traffic well past midnight, then, in the deep hours, when even late-carousing visitors and college students have had too much of the City That Care Forgot, the cars steadily, steadily sliding by, almost sotto voce, through the shadowy trees of dreams.

Do you know what it means / To miss New Orleans?" goes the song, with the Yankee pronunciation, because most English verse is naturally iambic or anapestic, and even if that were not the case, there is no way by which English could furnish a rhyme to the local pronunciation of the city name, which is drawn out or half-swallowed, with the accent on the *Or*, and is sometimes given the pseudo-folk spelling of "Nawlins." In any case, even here in Louisiana, the accent is sometimes put on the last syllable of the word: the avenue of that name is so pronounced, and, more importantly, the name of the parish, which is identical in geography to the city and, by constitutional provision, is charged with some aspects of its administration but does not share the same pronunciation. Even a third way of saying the name can be heard, if you know women who are members of the Orléans Club, which uses an approximation of the French pronunciation. I must confess to not minding the wrong pronunciation too much anyway. Arriving back in New York from Europe one summer, and waiting for the Crescent in Penn Station, I was pleased to hear called out the long litany of its stops, ending with the flourish of "New Orl*eens*."

In one sense, I cannot quite know what it means to

miss this city, since I live here—and have lived here now for nearly thirty-five years. How can you miss what you see, what you are? Popular wisdom has it that you never know how much you'll miss something until it's gone. As Sartre observed in *Psychology of the Imagination*, perception excludes imagination; you don't see a thing and call it up as an image at the same time. But some-times—as even he would agree—there is an absence at the heart of presence, death felt at the core of life, and nostalgia for what one has not yet lost. And the way one plays with death in sleep, I have played with separation, by spending long weeks and months away. Moreover, my acquaintance with New Orleans is not simply the unreflective contact of the quotidian; it is layered, com-posed of variegated strata of feeling and seeing, strata of past time (with which we are in contact—or I should not be writing this—and yet which is gone, and thus can be missed). Place is not only a metaphor for the self: it can be the self objectified, including the self of years ago.

It isn't, though, that I was stricken with love for the city from my first visits. For such an affective fire to flame up, circumstances must be propitious—and they were not particularly. In fact, all of my early stops in New Orleans had something disquieting or anguishing about them, and if New Orleans is the City That Care Forgot, it can also pull you down into its depths. Some who cast their lot here end up in a moral or material decadence that has none of the charm for which the place is justly famed. Others discover the slow, burning hurt that comes when happiness collapses into its hol-low core.

My initial visit to the Crescent City took place in the late 1950s, when I was married to my first husband and living in Houston. At the time, a sister of his, whom I shall here call Leo (for Leontine), lived here because her husband was employed by the Falstaff Brewery, now defunct. We had planned a visit—my first meeting—

around Thanksgiving. The day or so before we were to depart, I came home to find my husband huddled on the couch, wearing a red-and-white quilted bathrobe of mine, and looking ashen—certainly in no condition to travel. He had been taken ill at work with a collapsed lung and had been briefly hospitalized, then sent home with strict orders to rest and especially to lay off the cigarettes.

He had been a heavy smoker since his teens. What is it that has made me love repeatedly men who are addicted to tobacco, alcohol, or both? It is, I suppose, some addiction in me—a phenomenon my mother later identified, roughly, when she observed somewhat wearily that I always chose men with problems. Her remark was not meant, doubtless, as corrective, merely diagnostic; I was thirty-six at the time, and it was too late. I knew, of course, what she was thinking of. I could have answered that she herself had married a neurotic who felt the human burden keenly and lived in existential pain. (After all, who had quit one job after another and gone from place to place, even planning, the autumn he died, a new move?—when indeed he made one, but not the one he had planned. Who would sit with his head buried in his hands as he listened to symphonies and piano concertos by Mozart—the late ones—and Beethoven? Who stayed up most of the night reading Malraux's *Man's Fate* after I sent it to him, and found the recorded version of Samuel Beckett's *Waiting for Godot* too painful to bear?)

I also could have replied to Mother that the only interesting men, as far as I was concerned, were those with problems, or that only they would be willing to deal with me—who, in turn, given my maverick nature and temperamental complexity, could, if not mirror a problematic self, at least reasonably be expected to endure it. In any case, among the mistakes that I have most certainly made cannot be counted the supposition that I could have been happy for a lifetime—hardly for an evening—with one of those bland types who come out of a mold, no matter how respectable it might be (Presbyterian Church, Boy Scouts), and spend the flower of their youth preparing to return to it in their adulthood as clones of their fathers.

My first husband surely did not follow that pattern. He came from a decent but somewhat impoverished background—a family in St. Louis in which the father, an Irish immigrant, had died during the Depression from tuberculosis (an aftereffect of being gassed in the Great War) and the mother worked very hard to support her three children, on occasion scrubbing floors to make ends meet. The son, who was very able, had gone to work at age fifteen and never stopped, holding various jobs—railroad section laborer, fireman, brewery chemist, and riverboat hand, right on the river that I now see from my windows. He tried out a small college in Missouri, subsequently got to Texas, and put himself through the Rice Institute, first on a Naval ROTC scholarship, then later, when he was expelled from that program, by doing construction on Rice Stadium and ultimately working forty hours a week at Hughes Tool Company, on the other side of town. (The reasons for his expulsion from the ROTC were never divulged to me, probably for good cause, yet I suppose they would not have made much difference, for by the time the issue arose between us, love had done its work.)

He had subsequently been drafted into the army and, with the usual military miscalculation, was sent to France because he knew some German. He returned to Rice in 1954 to begin graduate studies in mathematics, with the express idea of becoming a professor, and after we became engaged, he spoke as if sharing the academic life with me in the future went without saying. Somehow, without telling me so, one semester after our marriage he simply dropped out of the graduate program, to my later incomprehension and dismay. Explain it as you will; perhaps, in fact, he had different dreams from mine and was less suited to the university than to industry, where he had a very successful career. Or was my single-mindedness in my own studies a burden to him? The causes of one's actions are often like hidden springs whose seepage is gradual but which finally may become visible as rivulets or soft, spongy ground; even then, their precise origin may remain uncertain. In any case, at this remove it is not a question of casting blame, merely of identifying a difference. We were in fact greatly different from each other. A feature article on him in a 2001 issue of the Houston *Chronicle* identified him as the very type of the left-brained person, whose idea of recreation is to attempt to solve mathematical problems; the only art that interests him is music. I, in contrast, though capable of doing well in the science and math courses of Rice's rigorous undergraduate curriculum, became focused then, as I remain, on words and their products.

To return to the New Orleans trip: when I arrived home that day, I found a smoker who was probably suffering withdrawal symptoms and who could barely breathe—a man accustomed to health and to dominating others (he was tall and well built) who was reduced to dependency. The sight was not comforting. It was decided, however, that we would go ahead and make the trip to New Orleans; I would drive, and he could rest in the backseat of our Chevrolet sedan, a spacious, high-built vehicle. The drive took about a day; Interstate 10 had not yet been built, and old Highway 90 took us along a route that served numerous little towns. By the time we were on the road, a Gulf Coast deluge that lasted the day long had settled in. In Orange, right near the state line, where the streets were flooded and waves made by passing pickups and boats slapped at the car doors, I navigated (the term is appropriate) through high water that today would immobilize anything except trucks and SUVs. Somehow, I made it through, apprehensive each minute and a sorry case of nerves. The nicotine-deprived passenger in the rear, biting at a hangnail, doubtless felt no better.

Then we were into Louisiana, with its long stretches of marsh and swamp that must be crossed on bridges. If you have ever driven over the old Louisiana causeways, built under the Huey P. Long administration—or, for that matter, the newer ones—picture them in a ceaseless downpour, with slanting rain blown violently at the windshield and lightning and thunder like cymbals and timpani on the nerves. Then imagine the Chevrolet creeping along as if it might be sucked into the swamps, the gray concrete sidings of the bridge disappearing into the gray of the water, swamp, and sky, so that, like a pilot in a whirlwind, one lost the horizon; picture me peering through the streaming windshield and the passenger gnawing himself (as the French say for "worrying"—except that in this case it was literal).

The last ordeal was the Huey P. Long Bridge. This structure is sturdy, apparently, since it has lasted for decades, despite having its lower structure rammed frequently by wayward barges and tankers piloted (or rather, *not* piloted) by intoxicated captains. But it was intended for small vehicles of an earlier decade, not the large sedans popular in the late 1950s. I found myself threading along a narrow lane, with trucks to one side of me and, to the other, below a railing that looked as flimsy as a picket fence, the swirling waters of the rain-swollen Mississippi. Since that trip, I have rarely crossed that structure by car, and never happily; at least when I used to ride the Southern Pacific's Sunset Limited going to Texas, I could close my eyes. Now, from the rooftop deck of the Garden District high-rise where I live, I have a better way to appreciate the undeniable grace of that bridge; barring fog, I can see upriver across the steeples and higher buildings of Uptown all the way to the "parish" (Jefferson Parish) and Long's namesake bridge.

What I first saw of New Orleans was a suburb—no improvement over anything in Houston. My sister-in-law and her spouse were not my kind of people. On weekends, he drank the product of his brewery from morning until whiskey time, and he liked coarse jokes. No appreciation for his adopted city seemed to have taken root in him. Leo had a terrible temper; she would rage for a while, slam the door, get in the car, and disappear for hours. What they thought of me I can now imagine—an intellectual, a snob, a prude, hopelessly sheltered, living in a rarefied world. Doubtless at the conclusion of our marriage, if not of our visit, they gave free rein to their opinions. At this remove, other details of the visit are far from clear. My husband must have started feeling better; at least we visited the French Quarter and Canal Street and saw the river. Whether we took a steamboat ride I cannot recall. One of our stops was Pat O'Brien's, which I had heard about in college from a few men students who came over on weekends seeking thrills unavailable around Rice. The hurricane cocktail I ordered was, until sometime in the 1990s when two students invited me there for an end-of-semester celebration, the only one I had ever drunk. We also went to a Schwegmann's Giant Supermarket, doubtless less as a tourist attraction than because Leo needed groceries; strangely, it is among the places I remember best, for the markets I patronized in the Village area of Houston, even so-called supermarkets, were outdone by this sprawling business. As for the departure from New Orleans and the trip back to Texas, they are not even shadows in my mind. Yet, except for a shaky start, the stay with the in-laws, and the stop at Schwegmann's, my first visit here was like that of hundreds of thousands of other visitors—French Quarter, bars, restaurants—and the tourists usually go home pleased, having seen things, drunk and eaten things, and done God knows what else that they do not indulge in regularly in Kansas City, Tulsa, or Minneapolis. (My father associated New Orleans chiefly with yellow fever and malaria, but to most people it represents pleasure and dreams—the dreams, as so often, taking the form of dissipation, imprudent behavior, or downright evil.)

A very few years afterward, we again came to New Orleans, again in a cold rain, for the Sugar Bowl game between Rice and Ole Miss. Finding nothing closer, we were obliged to stay at a motel in Houma, a town I have only once set foot or wheel in since and which I now consider remote, although in fact one can drive there easily (New Orleans provincialism *should* be as legendary as that of New York). I remember Claiborne Avenue— clogged, not like a bayou with wild iris, but with cars— and the lake-damp wind blowing through the bleachers of old Tulane Stadium. Later, I lived for many years within a short walking distance of where we sat that day; and, before the old structure was replaced as a foot- ball venue by a state-owned (if barely stately) down- town pleasure dome, which looks like a mushroom or the top of a giant roll-on deodorant, I went to a number of Saints games there, including the 1970 contest when Tom Dempsey kicked his last-minute sixty-three-yard field goal. (Unlike most of those in attendance earlier, I did not miss it, since once I go anywhere—show, game, party—I usually stay till the end.) From the Sugar Bowl game, I also remember my new tan trench coat, a green blouse that had been put under the Christmas tree a week before, and some perfume—Chanel No. 5—a gift from my husband. The gestures we each made were, however, powerless; our marriage was moving toward its end. Perhaps it is the memory of the perfume, and an occasional Proustian whiff of it, that throw over that visit a sense of failure that cannot be forgotten.

How would New Orleans have appeared to me if I had never returned? Would it have seemed irreparably associated with vague anxieties, a leaden feeling in the heart, and churlish weather? Or would it, with time, have turned into what it is for many, another manifes- tation of the shimmering maya of the mind? Whatever the case, the image of the city gradually assumed other dimensions. Once, coming through from Texas to Florida, I stopped overnight, between trains, at the Roosevelt

Hotel (now Fairmont), just as a hurricane was threatening the Gulf Coast. I sat in the Sazerac Bar keeping up with the weather reports, not knowing that a friend in Florida, expecting me the next day, was anxiously ringing my room, fearful that the train would not run. But it did, and when I arrived in Lake City I was greeted by a warm embrace and a gale that tossed the pines and palm fronds like my cascading hair.

On another occasion, when I was still living in Virginia but preparing to settle in New Orleans, I got on the Southerner in Charlottesville—with help, for I was as sick as a person can be while still managing to keep upright; food poisoning had hit shortly before, and before boarding I had left the women's room of the station in an appalling condition. Throughout most of the ride, approximately twenty-four hours, I had lain in my roomette in waking agony or sleeping delirium. Fortunately, toward the end a marked improvement had set in, and in the final minutes of daylight I had been able to watch with pleasure the moon-white glaze of Lake Pontchartrain turn dark silver. I stayed at the Columns Hotel, then a rather shabby shared-bathroom place, before it acquired a bar, valet parking, and national cachet; it has now become my club, so to speak, since I have drinks on the veranda there, alone or with friends, several times a month. The inn was then managed by a busybody who, doubtless as a test for her client, vaguely suspect though with a Virginia address, offered opinions I did not need on New Orleans neighborhoods (read: racial questions). I recall on that visit walking along St. Charles Avenue behind a man who obscurely reminded me of Marcel Proust's Baron Charlus and, upon overtaking him, discovering with dismay that it was someone I had met before, whose "orientation" (as it now would be put), surely despite and unbeknownst to him, revealed itself from the rear. To this bit of local color was added the Southern Gothic flavor of an apartment I considered renting, on St. Charles but metaphorical miles from the architectural and horticultural beauty that characterizes most sections of that avenue. The dingy edifice, managed by an old woman in a wheelchair and her unshaven, beady-eyed, whiskey-breathed, middle-aged son, would have satisfied the busybody of the Columns because it is just within the Garden District, thus a respectable address, but it was too decadent for me.

Now, nearly thirty-five years later, I can see, if I look left from my windows on Second Street, that same avenue, with its oaks and streetcars, or, looking right, the trace of the river beyond the trees, sweeping in its broad crescent upstream to the Harmony Street wharf and downstream to find its channel under the twin bridges, straight ahead from me, which cross to and from Algiers (the bridges did not exist when I first drove here). Tonight, a curl of moon like orange peel hangs over the pink steeple of Trinity Church, but clouds have not parted elsewhere, and the towers of St. Alphonsus and St. Mary's Assumption Churches in the Irish Channel and the great fungous Superdome on Poydras are just barely visible at the line where hovering darkness meets garlands of city lights. Leaning over my railing, I must try to imagine what it means to miss this city—for those born here, or for someone recently stricken with love for it, or for somebody like me, whose attachment is old and deep, and whose practical, affective, literary, intellectual life has long been played out, after uncertain beginnings, among its trees and narrow streets and cultural ghosts, where the scale of things still seems to be compatible with our desires.

Water is very much on my mind this late-spring day, after what the meteorologists called a "train" of thick black clouds formed to the southwest and settled over New Orleans and the rest of southeast Louisiana this past Monday, dumping its load and redumping the next day as the overladen clouds burst again, finally emptying twenty-four inches of rain at some locations across Lake Pontchartrain and eighteen inches at my place in the Garden District. For a sunken, marshy city that is mostly below sea level—a city where pumps, some of them relics of the nineteenth century, must replace gravity as draining agents, drawing the wet stuff into canals, thence into already swollen lakes, bayous, and rivers—this is no petty event.

Water seeks its level; and here it is a great leveler, and not just of terrain, as it erodes irregularities and spreads alluvial soils. The less prosperous residents of Harvey and Marrero on the West Bank, or of Kenner near the airport, or of the lower portions of St. Bernard, St. Charles, and St. Tammany Parishes, where swamps were solidified just enough to allow developers to get signatures on contracts for modest dwellings—these folk have once again been flooded out, with three or four feet of water in their houses and cars filled to the dashboards. Some of them had been through the same thing exactly one month ago, a lesser flood but enough to ruin the carpet, installed perhaps after a previous inundation, and to soak things in the garage. But the identical thing happens also to families who have fashionable addresses on Nashville and Jefferson Avenues in Uptown, whose "basements" (ground-level areas for storage, dens, or children's rooms) easily can take on three feet of water; and there are no fewer flooded cars along the most elegant parts of St. Charles Avenue than in many neighborhoods of lesser cachet.

In the deluge of May 3, 1978, when eleven inches fell in a short time, an acquaintance of mine rode his freezer (not *rowed*, however—no oar) on the choppy water of his basement. Another Uptowner I know has just started cleaning up this morning after his fourteenth inundation. Friends keep telling him to sell his place and move to a high-rise, perhaps the one where I now live, but since he is an honest man, selling is not facilitated by these repeated drenchings. Countless other Uptown residents I know have lost their cars and other possessions. The difference between them and the unfortunate people who bought affordable properties in such too aptly named areas as the River Vista subdivision across Lake Pontchartrain or Lake Estates upriver is that my friends have the resources to dig themselves out of the sludge and to replace what the waters consumed.

This year, when the rains started ("Chance of thunderstorms," the weatherman had said at 5:20—the same forecast given most evenings in spring and summer), I was in the Crêpe Nanou Restaurant, a very good French place on Robert Street between Prytania and St. Charles Avenue, with two students, one of whose academic success we were celebrating a few days before commencement (her Ph.D. was to be conferred shortly). It had already started raining some time before we were to meet. After we were seated, a populous *corps de ballet* of water drops began to dance down the front windows, nerve-knocking *basso profundo* thunder interrupted our conversation, and virtuoso performances by lightning were reflected in the tall mirrors. But, come, this is New Orleans: one is not deterred by rain. We continued our meal at a civilized pace. Dinner was nearly over, and we were just about to order the *crêpes marron* for dessert when nature decided to turn off the electricity; there went the chance for a dessert cooked to order. No matter. We paid by candlelight and made ready to leave. Robert Street was already flooded. Pascale, who was dressed in slacks, having originally planned to come by bicycle, brought around Melanie's car and drove right onto the sidewalk, so that the two of us wearing good dresses and high heels could step in nimbly close to the restaurant door. Perhaps, we thought, we can go for dessert to the Qué Será, where a new pastry chef who perfected his trade in Paris keeps urging us to taste his wares. Down St. Charles, however, the water got deeper; the Qué Será was in a pond, inaccessible. *Qué será, será.*

Well, we would go to my place and eat leftover cake from the Winn-Dixie supermarket. Melanie's low-slung red Toyota could not handle St. Charles any further. We switched to Prytania Street and churned our way through the waves, riding the high middle of the street, barely getting past Touro Infirmary and through the sunken intersection at Louisiana Avenue. On Second Street, Melanie parked her car on the sidewalk—at a sufficient remove, we supposed, from the street currents—and we went up to my apartment on the seventh floor, whence we had a splendid view of lightning beyond the twin bridges across the Mississippi, rain shooting at us horizontally, and steadily rising water, soon sidewalk-high, visible (even after the streetlamps and every other light in a 180-degree arc went out) in the flashes, bright as dawn.

The upshot of the evening was that the girls spent the night with me, we had no electricity for twelve hours, and three days later, the Toyota, undrivable, has just

been hauled off, along with thousands of similarly dere-
lict vehicles. Others had much worse experiences and
lived to tell of them, and at least six have died. More,
most likely. Some vagrants whom no one misses probably got carried away. Moreover, during floods it is easier
than usual to get rid of someone you don't want—taking advantage of, or provoking, helplessness and then
dumping the body into a watery grave, not even both-
ering to drive to St. Charles or St. James Parish to throw
it into the swamp.

Yet this unwanted water, which has reappeared in
salty form on the cheeks of some as they survey their
disappearing gardens and sodden floors, and contem-
plate the loss of many of their worldly goods, is a vital
liquid, one of the elements to which we owe life. In the
beginning, God's spirit moved upon the waters. We are
told by evolutionists that land-based life evolved from
the sea. A human embryo, cradled in its insulating liquid, goes through its fish stage; such early features as the
gill-like pharyngeal slits, which as the fetus matures turn
into other structures, including the middle ear, underline our kinship with the finny tribe. Baptism by fire
through the Holy Spirit may be the supreme sign of
cleansing and renewal, but most of us are fit only for a
lesser experience, which water affords both symbolically
and practically. Saint John himself, perhaps one of the
baptizing Essenes, stood in the Jordan River, immersing
all those seeking purification, including the One whose
shoelaces he was not worthy to untie.

As a westerner, I remain fascinated with whatever
flows, and note that *flowing* is a pleasing quality in many
things, including dance gowns, landscapes, a starry train
in the firmament, conversation in a foreign tongue ("flu-
ency"), painting, sculpture, music, and prose. (I shall not
include "cash," as in "cash flow"; while favorable, the latter denotes nothing aesthetic.) Having learned to swim,
tardily, at age seventeen, I like to feel the waves of the
warm Gulf waters bathe me, one after the other. I enjoy

the broad prospect of the Mississippi River viewed from Audubon Park or near Jackson Square in the French Quarter; it is truly a continental artery, massive, totally unlike the streams I was once accustomed to, and as cultural as a natural feature can be. Fresh rain, by its sound and scent, delights me, as does the sight of clouds at the horizon with their burden scrimming down, highlighted by the sun's great spotlight. From the age of ten, when my family initially moved to Texas and I first saw the Gulf of Mexico, through my early crossings of the Atlantic (by the French liners *Flandre* and *Liberté*) and my first visits to the Mediterranean, to the time when I lived in Florida, to the long years here near the Mississippi Sound, I have been drawn to the sea, loving its freedom, finding its motions so much like my emotions. Some of my favorite poems concern the ocean—Paul Valéry's "Cemetery by the Sea," for instance, and Jules Supervielle's lyrics from his twenty-two ocean crossings between Europe and South America. I have even special affection for music with the theme of water—Debussy's *La Mer,* Ravel's *Jeux d'eau,* Mendelssohn's *Calm Sea and Prosperous Voyage,* and especially Handel's *Water Music,* which I have known since childhood but never enjoyed more than at a concert in an amphitheater in Greece, not far from the archetypical Homeric sea, which is the source of so much of the literary imagination.

A generous spring storm never hits here without my thinking of western ranchlands such as those of the Big Bend, where, after a few years back in Colorado, my parents settled permanently. There, the cult of rain equals that which we read about among the native peoples of the Southwest, with their careful channeling of mesa rivulets and their elaborate rituals intended to draw the life-giving liquid from the will of the gods and the clouds' abundance. My father watered our trees from crystalline wells, returning to the ground at selected spots, for our pleasure and the earth's adornment, what the ground had given. For Big Bend ranchers who came into town to get the mail or supplies, it was more than casual talk to compare rainfall amounts for the season—a contest usually won by those who ranched north of Alpine, in or near the Davis Mountains, which catch what moisture there is, leaving for the others nothing but dry rumblings of thunder and a streaked sky in the distance.

Preposterous though it be, the wish sometimes forms in me to ship out our superfluous Louisiana storms for my *compañeros* in Texas and elsewhere in the West, to whom a little would mean much. I have read that projects have been conceived to convey water from the Columbia River down to California by means of a gargantuan ocean-floor pipeline. The scheme of transporting rain from New Orleans is still more harebrained. And in truth, of course, the West could not accept such largesse, or at least not in the quantities we have at our disposal. The soil here is spongy, used to being soaked, and protected by plants, and we have canals and ditches dug expressly for overflow. But two inches can fill a West Texas arroyo, and a twenty-inch rain in an arid land would swell the rivers and inundate dry creekbeds; cover roads and pastures; drown antelope, cattle, sheep, goats, and horses on the range; carry off the sparse and precarious, if spiny, vegetation and what little topsoil has been left by the winds; ruin many dwellings, adobe or frame; and, as when the town of Sanderson was half destroyed, take the lives of many who make a difficult living from a dry world. Years ago, the Pecos River bridge on U.S. Highway 90, built solidly into the black rock well above water level, was carried away when the canyon was flooded by downpours that the desert ranges could not absorb. If the replacement bridge—at the level of the high edges—ever is washed out, much of West Texas will go also.

Meditating on these matters, one observes that the scope of human needs, capacity, and endurance is in fact extremely narrow. Between the shriveling of plant life and the painful death of sentient beings through deprivation of water, on the one hand, and, on the other, a surfeit sufficient to destroy vegetation and drown most animal life (or at least inconvenience it mightily) runs the strip of possibility. In the early 1930s, Antoine de Saint-Exupéry nearly drowned when his plane crashed into the Mediterranean. A few years later, he came close to dying again after his engine failed and he was downed in the Libyan desert, when he and his mechanic were forced to endure nearly five days without liquid, having salvaged from their airplane only a little coffee, a liter of wine in a thermos, a few grapes, and an orange. They were rescued when, hallucinating and barely conscious, they stumbled into the path of a solitary Bedouin—simply "man," as Saint-Exupéry called him.

Composed mostly of H_2O, we require it but still cannot handle much of it unless it is confined or we are insulated from it. The same limitations obtain with heat, and cold, and sunlight, and a host of other things. The Greeks, while sensitive to what they (and I) see as man's proper place and home in the natural world, recognized these limitations, among others, and would have considered it hubris to ignore them and violate the rule of moderation. "Nothing to excess," one of them said. (Yet Gide claimed, "Extremes touch me." But he had in mind *human* extremes, *human* dimensions, not the extremes of the physical world, familiar to most of our species and to which science has introduced us further in a dizzying fashion.) We all navigate a narrow channel between too shallow and too deep. Let the pillows in the hotel not be thick and hard, or I shall not sleep at all; on the other hand, I want *something* substantial between my head and the mattress. We cannot really take *anything*, not even our greatest delights, except in moderate quantities. With its extremes of temperatures and its inconceivable magnitude of astrophysical activities, distance, and time, we barely belong in this universe. In this sense, certainly, if in no other, we are strangers to the cosmos. "My field is time," said Goethe. But except in relation to that of the microworld—the *ciron,* or mite, to which the philosopher Pascal contrasted the boundless heavens—this time is so greatly limited as to resemble a rivulet on which a child guides a paper boat, streaming eventually into the flooded plain of infinity. And of our time, only the middle portion, between dependent childhood and frail old age, is of much use—the high ground, like that hump on which Melanie steered the red Toyota through the waters of Prytania Street.

When Robert Frost wondered whether the world would end in fire or ice, perhaps he should have added water as a third alternative. After all, according to the Hebrew Scriptures, God's first generalized act of wrath against his rebellious creation was by water; geological and archaeological evidence offers considerable support for the prototypical flood. Certainly, the liquid element once covered much more of the planet than at present: fossilized shells are found in landlocked mountainous regions, and calcareous layers in high altitudes are the residue of innumerable sea organisms. We have had abundant intimations recently that the earth may be returning to this aqueous state. *Après nous, le déluge.* This is especially true where human beings have meddled in things as much as they have in South Louisiana—innumerable levees built by the Army Corps of Engineers, the state, and the New Orleans Levee Board; marshes drained to make way for asphalt; trees felled; and, most particularly, the Mississippi River turned aside from the channel it clearly *wishes* to take, through the Atchafalaya Basin, and obliged for the moment to follow the course we have chosen for it. In a few millennia, maybe centuries, even if these acts of interference were all reversed, this part of the world might be underwater anyway. We are told that the greenhouse effect, brought about by thinning of the ozone layer through our overproduction of carbon dioxide and the spewing of fluorocarbons from aerosol cans and such, will so warm the earth that the polar ice caps will melt and crumble at the edges, thereby raising ocean levels over the entire planet and possibly flooding coastal areas on almost every continent, including the East Coast population centers, almost the entirety of Florida (high point 345 feet), and all of South Louisiana.

These last few days, some of us may have become islands in a postdiluvian sea, a sea that, like almost everything else, is expansionist, seeking to rejoin its brethren the Mississippi, the lakes (Pontchartrain, Catherine, Borgne, Maurepas, Salvador, Des Allemands), the swamps, and the bayous, all of which soon may be joined, taking us with them, in a vast, embracing union. (In the Venetian Republic, the Doge used to be "wed" annually to the sea, in a ceremony fraught with cultural and anthropological meanings.) But islands we are not. Donne doubtless had something else in mind, but what he said applies here anyway. Snowmelt and rain upstream swell the rivers here and flood towns in between, toxic chemicals from the "Cancer Corridor" between Baton Rouge and New Orleans run downstream and poison marine life, acid rain and surface pollution have made parts of the Great Lakes moribund. Evil, doubtless, spreads even more certainly, if insidiously. Our degraded ethical practices and civic and moral flaws reach others by contagion, not merely spreading, but worsening, in a serial fashion by which reactions produce expanded counterreactions. This week, in a different, and heartening, illustration of solidarity, many people, including some of very modest station, have given to flood victims they do not know their support in the form of friendship and money. The term is "outpouring" of generosity—a flow from the human spirit that recognizes the predicament of fellows.

There is still another sort of connectedness, that to our primitive ancestors, whose ties with the natural world were so much more closely and constantly knit than ours, and to those less remote dwellers in the eastern Mediterranean, with their mythologies of nature into which they wove also the human dream of the supranatural, each penetrating the other. We dream of everything that is impossible, imagining that we have other faculties, living other lives, being what and where we are not; and some of those dreams involve intimacy with and mastery over nature in the form of its four elements, which, by virtue of their very contrasts, come to mind as a cluster, the idea of water calling forth its complements of earth, air, and fire. Their mythological embodiments still have a place in our literary imagination. Hermes sped about the earth with a winged helmet and heels, Icarus flew on wings of feathers and wax toward the heavens, the steeds of Helios crossed the sky each day, and Pegasus rose ultimately to the place of the gods. Descending into the earth itself, Orpheus and Persephone visited the underworld. Various mythological birds and salamanders, dwelling in fire, expressed the unrealizable vision of being burnt and refined to purity without being destroyed; the phoenix rises from its ashes. Thanks to the whale's body, Jonah dwelt in the seas, and Poseidon, along with naiads, Nereids, and many others, incarnated the human desire to live in and exercise sovereignty over the water. Some myths seem to unite all these archetypes. Zeus, born in a cave, dwelt in the Olympian ether, distributed rain, and hurled lightning bolts as the heavens stormed. Through syncretism, presumably, they are all found in the Christian corpus: Christ was baptized and walked on water; the Holy Spirit descended in tongues of fire; after a descent into hell—the underworld—Christ ascended into the heavens (he "rises better than aviators and holds the world's record for height," wrote Guillaume Apollinaire in "Zone").

As any child will tell you who dreams of going to the center of the earth or twenty thousand leagues under the sea, these old desires, projected onto myth, have not disappeared. Planes and submarines have brought material realization to some of them, in a way; but although these constructions are useful, they are not truly the dream. With the arrival of men on the moon, an enduring desire for cosmic travel, appealing to our body-bound psyche, has been turned into a technological matter—an impressive feat, no doubt, but which, done in the name of science, finally narrows rather than widens the range of the imagination. Fantasy is all: these elemental attractions say something about our origins and some very basic attachments. At the outset of this collection, and again in this essay, I have mentioned my special liking for water. In memory, I can still see, hear, and feel bubbling the cold creeks of the Colorado mountains of my childhood—little Redskin Creek near my grandmother's cabin, merely a pace wide, which we used as a refrigerator by placing an immense crock among the pebbles, and Vasquez Creek and the Gunnison River where, later, I went fishing with my father. But I also have a feeling for air—the wind coming across the range, the invisible movement of high currents driving clouds, or an airy evening on the porch, all windows open; and for earth—a cool pine-needle bed under the ponderosas, or the sandy soils of the Big Bend, shaded from burnt red to yellow, tan, and chalky white—or stones, common stones; and for fire, perhaps outdoors, after a meal, or in a country house in winter, an invitation to fellowship or lovemaking.

Much of this is connected not just to origins—the water we came from, the land that received us, the air we breathe, the warming hearth of our primitive cave homes—but to ends. We all have fantasies of returning to the breast of the earth, of seeing the world purified by refiners' fires. I never forget my uncle Jack, who died in the Battle of Leyte Gulf in the Philippines in October 1944 and was committed to the waves ("Die at sea, lie at sea"). In Isaiah's words, "The earth shall be full of the knowledge of the Lord, as the waters cover the sea." Despite the wrath of biblical deluge, this eschatological vision refreshes us: doubtless all but the most corrupt, the truly evil, thirst after righteousness, though they may not know it. The French word *crue*, meaning the level of flood waters, is identical to a term for *growth* and is connected to *cru*, "crop or vintage"—all from *croître*, "to increase"—as though we could not progress, nor the earth develop, without these vital, overflowing waters that make plains and valleys fertile and nourish our souls.

Unlike many nineteenth-century writers, however, I do not wish, on the basis of these reflections about nature and human experience, to elucidate further the relationship between them, or to connect them to the mind of God. Closer to the phenomenologists, I *observe*—seeing the limitations of this observation, and the impossibility, whether through science or poetry, of going beyond it. Water *is*. The rest is our human embroidering. Even though I see my own freedom in images of water—the swiftness of a mountain stream, the easy and rhythmic motion of waves, the vast perspective of the ocean inviting our mind to embrace what it will—the feeling cannot be traced beyond these images and my inner, unprovable conviction that it is there. Yet if I were absolutely obliged to draw ontological conclusions concerning nature, they would be pantheistic. Surely, the conviction that God, or some other cosmic power, is everywhere, even in nature's destructiveness, is no less worthy than that which posits a benevolent, all-wise deity who nevertheless allows the existence of evil. Of course, I do not set this forth as a theology; it is more a disclaimer.

Three full days after the flood waters receded, the New Orleans skies are generally overcast. We have had more cloudbursts, happily of short duration. More than once, the sun has shown a bit of its face, though it has never entirely pushed aside the lumpy gray curtain, whether through unwonted timidity or through shame at having let itself be eclipsed so long by a mere storm. After many hours of absence (the tracks were impassable), the streetcars are once more running on St. Charles Avenue, their music of motors, rails, and bells making sleep possible again. The meteorologists predict fair weather for the weekend. *Après la pluie, le beau temps,* says plainly the French proverb, in an oblique recognition that human fate too, while changeable and unpredictable, usually provides some blessings after great trials. The wheel of fortune turns, as does the world, and imbalances frequently are righted, one way or another.

Some imbalances cannot, however, be redressed by any act of man, and among them is, almost surely, the repeated flooding of New Orleans and surrounding areas. This spot attracted the early explorers because they found an easy portage route from the Mississippi to Bayou St. John, which flows into Lake Pontchartrain, giving efficient access to the Gulf of Mexico, which was otherwise still more than a hundred miles downstream. The facility of water trade was what led to the development of a city. But surely it was unwise to presume as much since then as we have with respect to nature, destroying the natural drainage of marshlands by paving open spaces, dredging bayous, and constructing dikes—those built as such and those known as roads—and other measures by which we redesign the natural topography. Marshes will not return where subdivisions have sprung up like mushrooms. One might object that without subdivisions many would have nowhere to live. But distant suburbs have created as many problems as they have solved—perhaps more—and by no means have they guaranteed individual happiness. If we could oblige bankers and developers to cease proclaiming that the "American dream" is to own a separate dwelling surrounded by expanses of grass, we might be able to persuade people to return to the cities that so many have forsaken and to live in structures that save space—high-rise buildings, garden apartments, and townhouses.

Having thus taught us again this week the disadvantages, indeed the dangers, of redesigning nature, water at the same time has underlined our solidarity and given, to some at least, an experience of sharing that suggests how a few remedies might be devised in common. Perhaps the lesson is not quite over: as I look out my windows toward the avenue, I see a field of umbrellas suddenly popping open, like flowers in a cartoon. "On such a full sea are we now afloat," as Brutus says in *Julius Caesar,* that we can't absorb much more. But above the geminate bridges over the Mississippi, bright rays that pierce the clouds are transforming the rain into a dazzling screen of light, and the watery roofs and spires around me have turned to silver.

ike Rousseau, who gave advice in *Emile* on the education of children while abandoning to foundling hospitals those he begat with Thérèse Levasseur, I am going to write here on a topic for which, some might say, I am ill qualified or at least not licensed. Like many of the thousands of other terms in English that include particles, *getting along* is an interesting little verb, which must be distinguished from *getting by, getting on, getting away, getting away with . . . , getting with* [*it*]—one I wouldn't use—*moving along,* and various locative and performance expressions such as *getting up*. The *along* part suggests progress or movement through space or time, appropriate to the temporal dimension of human life. The French say *s'entendre*—"to understand one another"—a clearer expression than afforded by the Germanic *get* of the grounds of comprehension on which good relations are built, but less progressive.

Surely, I have no claim to have had smoother dealings than others with my fellow human beings or to have succeeded particularly well in the rocky, sometimes treacherous fields of human intercourse, especially marriage, and sometimes I've done worse than could have been hoped for; in addition, nothing certifies me professionally, unless you deem that, given much of its subject matter since the twelfth century, a broad acquaintance with French literature does constitute some informal credentials. But precisely as the ill are concerned with medicine and victims of crime and those involved in litigation have an uncommon interest in policing, law, and court proceedings, so I, as someone connected, willynilly, to others, have particular interest, as well as something at stake, in this business of getting along. And failure does not mean necessarily absence of ideas or ideals.

Moreover, many of those who have so-called credentials in the "getting along" business—I think of school and marriage counselors, "human relations" officers in industry and at universities, psychologists and psychiatrists, institutional sociologists, neo-Marxist critics—are half-charlatans, maladjusted, incompetent, sometimes crazies, no better placed (perhaps less well) than the rest of us to advise, and chiefly concerned with preserving or enhancing their clientele or position. The influence that they exercise over others is sometimes abusive and pathological, including the transference phenomenon between subject and analyst. As for celibate counselors, no matter how good their intentions, they are, I remain convinced, ill positioned to advise on conjugal matters, grave or mundane, beyond handing out truisms. Finally, I certainly am no less authorized to write, as I shall, on social matters, whether at the individual or community level, than are many self-proclaimed experts, such as those in the English or French departments at XYZ University who pronounce on capitalism, pornography, imperialism, "gender construction," and so forth.

This concern for getting along is notwithstanding the fact that now I live alone, with those I care about the most residing elsewhere and, having turned in my time card at Tulane for the last time, as readers know, so that I would have more opportunity and more freedom for other things, now am under no daily obligation, practically speaking, to get along with anyone. I could just become an old misanthropic curmudgeon and say "a plague on you all." But the other things for which I wished more time include other *people,* some known to me and nearby or easily reachable by highway or plane, others members of the anonymous crowds of life, about whom, after all, I am concerned, and to whom my writing is directed. (These others nearby include Paul Brosman, about whom a word is in order: he and I are no longer married, but I do not want to write him out of this book because he is not written out of my life. Far from it. We see each other at least twice a week, I prepare a hot meal at his house on Sunday evenings and share it with him, I get library books for him, and I assist him with typing and groceries and so on.) As the example of Swift is there to show, misanthropy does not exclude caring. The maxim attributed to Chamfort is apt: "He who is not a misanthrope at age forty has never loved mankind." Chamfort saw things very darkly indeed, not only for personal reasons: he watched the 1789 Revolution, to which he gave support, turn into the Terror; but he also saw well. Being removed does not preclude understanding others. Does the solitary lighthouse keeper not see better from his tower, and the sage or monk—even, perhaps, a prisoner—at his window not have a valuable perspective? The mind, apparently enclosed in itself, does, after all, look out through the windows of its eyes onto a vast arc of life.

In truth, I feel considerable benevolence toward my fellow human beings and am very much concerned about how they might manage to get along somewhat better, whether on a small scale, such as that of some former neighbors who had drunken disputes, or the larger one of, say, Northern Ireland, the Balkan nations, central Africa, Central Asia, or the Near East. Reading about their bloody conflicts and similar strife is always painful, but of course I have no means of reducing them in the least. I *can* occasionally do something on the micro-scale. My father could get along with almost anyone and was often an agent of calm and harmony; my mother worked on a personal and a community level—including the Spanish-speaking half of Alpine—toward such ends. Fortunately, they gave me some of their skills. A former provost of Tulane called me a "compromising woman" because I had been central in working out an accommodation to resolve a major departmental conflict. (That was in 1969. I suppose that now, if I chose, I could charge him with harassment for this sexual innuendo.) Adjustments, modifications, renunciations are essential in the process that human relations always are; sometimes, when we see one claim, one right ceaselessly being opposed by others, it seems as if successful human dealings must *all* be compromise. But of course there are instances when accommodation should not be made; error needs to be rooted out, not given half of the territory, and such various failings as wickedness, cruelty, indolence, irresponsibility, intolerance, mendacity, and false witness deserve no quarter, no appeasement. As for what Proust called the true sadism—indifference to the sufferings of others—it needs understanding and, if possible, correction.

Society, or collective life, strikes me as being, on a massive and awful scale, like marriage, although the latter is optional, whereas one enters social units in the first instance as a result of others' actions. Everyone except hermits is in a social network, usually with multiple layers or branches—needing it, as people seem to need their marriage, taking from it, giving back (one hopes). Society resembles marriage also in its amazing resiliency, but neither, of course, is proof against unraveling. When people get along, living or working together—spouses, friends, collaborators—they are to be congratulated, perhaps emulated, since their relationship benefits not only them and those close by but the larger social fabric. When thousands, nay millions, tens or hundreds of millions, manage to coexist without great strife and political divorce, it is more remarkable than the permanence of the constellations. Considering the scale and complexity of the social order in just my own city of a half-million (excluding its suburbs, which are in fact considerably more populous), and beyond that, in the state, the nation, and the world community, in which the United States is deeply and lastingly entangled, I marvel that things are not even worse.

The major issue now, of course, is race—is *still* race—and unfortunately so. Of necessity, then, I am concerned about what are called "good race relations" as part of the wider concern for human relations in general. Broadly speaking, in New Orleans they are reasonably good, if the standards for measure take into account any of the awful alienation and strife of the past, in the United States and elsewhere. Fundamental and greatly needed changes in law, followed by alterations in behavior and attitude on a wide scale and the coming to age of a generation that did not know the Jim Crow society, have transformed New Orleans, like much of the nation. (Little credit for this progress should be given, however, to the Great Society programs, which have replaced individual initiative with entitlements and have created cumbersome, self-serving bureaucracies.) Some who did not want to share these changes have moved to the suburbs, thus cutting themselves off from a city of great charm, tradition, spirit, and human warmth. So much the worse for them; it is a pity that their departure has significantly reduced the tax base.

Perhaps—except at the time of the nineteenth-century White League and during some moments in the 1950s—it was easier for this city than others to move toward integration. The existence here as early as the eighteenth century of the *gens de couleur libres,* or free people of color, a group with many propertied and educated members, made New Orleans different from the rest of the Deep South. Moreover, certain European traditions here may have contributed to a more coherent, less divided society than in most southern cities. There is today a large black middle class, some descended from the free people of color, others more recent additions to the class. Finally, the tradition of neighborhoods and the layout of the city, confined by its river, lakes, and marshes, making us all live closer to each other, were factors in creating a greater sense of community than elsewhere, it seems to me ("checkerboard" is better than "split down the middle"). And Mardi Gras, as it has developed in recent decades, is a force of coherence in the city; the efforts of former city councilwoman Dorothy Mae Taylor to dismantle some of it were ill advised.

To assert this is not to deny that tremendous urban problems face this city, and some of them have a racial dimension; but many should be called class problems instead, and although they have racial elements, it is a tactical mistake to view them only in those terms. It requires no sociological training—indeed, one is perhaps better off without some of its dogmas—to see that the social fabric here is not being torn apart by racial strife. On the contrary, in certain ways this fabric has strengthened, except at the level of the housing projects and other slums—that is, among the welfare and criminal classes.

The rest of us *have* to get along. Among those whites who remain and in the more numerous black community, one does not usually encounter great waves of racial resentment and hostility. Some on both sides, to be sure, are unreasonable; some are criminal. But in the streets and shops, customers, workers, and passers-by generally seem cordial enough to everyone, with little concern for skin color. Courtesy toward others is legendary here, and it usually works between races. The other day, a black man on the sidewalk behind me, walking faster even than I, passed me up, and in doing so turned to say, "You have very pretty gray hair." Clearly, he didn't resent me and supposed, rightly, that I would not resent him. Similarly, a black streetcar conductor said to me recently, as I was leaving his car, "Thanks, Sugar, and have a great evening"; a few years ago, another said, as

I got off in a cloud of French perfume, "I want to thank you for making my car smell so sweet."

In a recent poll, most respondents, black and white, acknowledged that they were satisfied with their lot. Human beings, despite their immense capacity for discontent, generally seem to like their little lives, and many show great understanding that the particular selves by which they came into and occupy a position in the world—sex, race, age, past and present circumstances—are, although contingent, a point of departure, a means that has both obliged and allowed them to fit themselves into life through their activity. Because of this appropriate activity, their lives now fit them. (I speak thus as a woman.) Montesquieu, the author of *The Spirit of Laws,* told of a poor man to whom a genie offered the chance to become someone else, proposing three apparently enviable conditions; the man declined them all. No one would agree to becoming someone else, Montesquieu concluded. In "La Mort du loup" ("The Death of the Wolf"), the Romantic poet Alfred de Vigny, at once an idealist and a pessimist, saw in these givens the way for a human being to reconcile himself with destiny:

> *Fais énergiquement ta longue et lourde tâche*
> *Dans la voie où le Sort a voulu t'appeler*
> [*Carry out energetically your long and heavy task*
> *In the path to which Fate has chosen to call you*]

It is no coincidence that Vigny's writings appealed to Albert Camus; their stoic and existentialist resonances announce *The Myth of Sisyphus.*

Something would be gained, I am convinced, if the terms in which urban progress is defined were not always racial and if the rhetoric of racism were put aside. The huge spreads in the New Orleans *Times-Picayune* that dramatize differences and feed victimization politics do more harm than good—except for those who *mean* to damage relations as part of their political strategy. To accuse us all of deep prejudice—as is done by countless orators, writers, and agitators of various sorts (especially university officials and those in institutions and programs whose raison d'être is the racial issue)—is not a service. At the least, it is unfair to many and useless to the others; it often does positive harm, as Thomas Sowell and other commentators have argued. It keeps red and raw the stigma (to use Shelby Steele's term) of being white, which is so easily attached to any North American of European extraction, although, whatever his antecedents, no one alive now was a slave-merchant in the colonies, and most have done nothing worse than profit a bit, indirectly and involuntarily, from their condition as white.

Moreover, those constantly accused of misdeeds become resentful. A 1993 poll reported by John M. Ellis in *Literature Lost* found that "young white adults are more biased against blacks than are their older counterparts." This is especially true in schools and on campuses where the institution itself adopts an accusatory posture and obliges staff and students to undergo sensitivity training, while following policies built on color distinctions. In a version of the self-fulfilling prophecy, the accused tend to identify with the image they are given of themselves. This was, of course, a generalized experience of blacks themselves in the years of scorn—the pre-emancipation, pre–civil rights periods. An instructive illustration of interiorizing an image is that of Jean Genet, the thief, thug, and jailbird who, thanks to considerable verbal gifts, his peculiar experience, and French indulgence for disorder, became a major French dramatist, poet, and novelist. A ward of the French state, placed in various foster homes and institutions, he was, as a boy, accused of theft; having a very precarious sense of self, he clutched onto that identity as a criminal and (at least as Sartre has analyzed his case) created his essence around it. The result was an original but highly antisocial personality who needed crime as a ratification of his being.

Of those charged indiscriminately with racism, let us hope that many more do not finally react to the point of fitting the label. It has happened already, to some degree, with members, especially male, of the white working class, in particular southern and rural (that is, Appalachians and rednecks, who are, with Texans, the only major groups that are still widely and legally mocked in films and television programs)—men who should feel much in common with others economically and socially disadvantaged but who have been stigmatized to the point of paranoiac hostility, at the same time as they see written into law special privileges for blacks and Hispanics. The development of militia and separatist groups is obviously not unrelated to this situation.

Much is distorted, furthermore, by the fear of appearing racist. At some universities, such fears have brought about virtual censorship of certain types of speech. On a more mundane level, in the Winn-Dixie checkout lines, I cannot make a pointed remark to a black woman who, leaving her little boys with her cart to hold her place in line, has gone to shop for a dozen or so additional items—a deliberate tactic for being close to the cash register by the time she has completed her purchases, so that, even though I really finished first, she is ahead of me. This obnoxious conduct deserves a reprimand, and I would be happy to give it to a white person: "Find everything you want before you get into line." "A la queue, à la queue!" people would yell out in France. But I cannot do so in this case for fear that the shopper will attribute my reproof to racial contempt—and thus I will contribute to deterioration of understanding—whereas really it is just contempt for anyone who does that.

At the other end of the spectrum, do black men and women think sometimes that my show of cordiality is not for them as individuals but for their race, a well-meant gesture perhaps but patronizing and demeaning? I hope not, but can I be sure of my own heart? Certainly, at least, I did not use a double standard in my teaching or other professional acts; the French, the analysis that is on the page, are what count, not the skin or other features of the person writing it. And I feel genuinely that these people whom I encounter at the Columns or in the Winn-Dixie or at a reception are my fellow New Orleanians, and we have much at stake, together. Sometimes I look upon living here as an extended camping experience: we retire to our tents separately at night, but activities of the day and concerns for our general welfare bind us together.

In short, I want equality before the law, before God, and reasonable efforts made to ensure this equality in practice and let it engender more equitable opportunities. Yet it will probably not surprise the reader that I do not favor set-asides, quotas, preferences, reparations, or any other means, open or concealed, by which anyone, as a member of a "group" (usually race, possibly sex or "sexual preference," or "disadvantaged"—in practice overlapping with race), receives any institutionalized special treatment. As Steele has argued in *The Content of Our Character,* and Sowell in *Inside American Education,* such preferences over recent decades have brought in their wake very serious ills, collective and individual, among them the creation of the victimization culture, the masking or devaluation of real achievement by those favored through special programs and the consequent frustration or self-doubt on the part of the competent, the preservation of color as a deciding factor in judgment, and the distortion of human relationships, which has led to new paternalism and new resentment. It is an ironic truth that the more any group relies on victimization rhetoric and concessions made in its name, the less well members of that group perform in competition with others. The defects in feminist thinking that Ellis identifies are similar to those in racist rhetoric: the belief that all failures are due to conspiracy and persecution "becomes yet another barrier to . . . progress."

Quotas and set-asides should thus be abolished in

contracting at both the governmental and private levels. School and university admissions and evaluations should be done solely on terms of academic merit determined by the familiar, traditional ways of gauging it, not some new formula eschewing standard objective measures. Hiring in government and other institutions, retentions, promotions, and so on should be on a color-blind basis. If a philanthropist wishes to endow scholarships through his own foundation or some other channel outside of the government and schools, that is grand, and he may give them to whom he wishes, on any basis; but any grant monies for students or faculty, no matter how raised, that are distributed through any public or quasi-public institution (such as a private university dependent upon public funds and tax exemption) should be awarded without regard for factors other than academic ones and financial need.

The Hopwood decision in Texas and Proposition 209 in California were thus a victory for reason and justice and ultimately for the nation. Agreeing on this are not only well-known blacks such as Sowell and Ward Connerly, but numerous others less known, as well as large numbers of whites who, like me, have truly liberal ideas, not what passes currently for such. A piece I have just read in *Heterodoxy* by Patrick Hall, a black professor from South Bend, speaks of an old math professor he had, a Jesuit, who made it plain that he demanded from him no less than from others—a good deal. "I know now he probably cared more for me as a human being than all the liberal educators have done with their paternalistic pandering to black students in recent decades." Hall rejects the "new educational quackery" based on so-called distinct African values and insists that identical standards be applied to all, regardless of socioeconomic background and race. When favoritism is ended and individual responsibility and performance resume their rightful place, we will be better off and, on the broad scale, get along much better.

Adversaries of my positions—if they have read this far—have already dismissed me, doubtless, as having an unreconstructed outlook, its ingredients bigotry, stupidity, bad faith, and traditionalism. To the most radical of opponents, there is no point in arguing my case further. To the more moderate ones, I shall appeal by saying that at least I live such convictions as I have, remaining in the city itself instead of taking advantage of my retirement to flee to the suburbs (or, as some liberal colleagues have, to a more enlightened state), walking the streets, taking the streetcar, going to restaurants and bars that have many black patrons, making my purchases here rather than at distant malls, never considering other races as "invisible"; for twenty-four years, I lived a block or so from a thick concentration of blacks, lower middle class at best—an experience that many of those with different views have not had. If this sounds smug, I hope to be forgiven. I trust, rather, that it is what Steele calls "a heartfelt feeling of concern without any compromise of one's highest values and principles."

A friend of mine speaks of the need for spouses to *affirm* each other (not the same, of course, as "affirmative action"). This approach, which can be extended to dealings with other family members and friends and trusted colleagues, assumes shared values and moral equality. Ideally, this outlook should be extended broadly throughout society; it is implied by the opening words of the Declaration of Independence and much subsequent legislation. Only what is of value should be affirmed, of course; I am not a relativist and cannot see how anyone can be. Does the radical *really* believe that all truth is "socially constructed," all texts equally valuable, and all habits acceptable? Is he truly persuaded that such cultural relativism or "diversity" will give equal voice to all and not produce tribal slaughter? Will he want any children he might have—and not abandon, like Rousseau, or, more likely, abort—to live according to this creed? Would he prefer that life be "nasty, brutish, and short" to "comfortable, enlightened, long and fulfilling"?

Good parents understand as a matter of course both values in general and the irreplaceable value of the child, who is a person, not a property, toy, or sign, and is to be heeded, nurtured, developed in his self even as he is directed, corrected, taught, and chastized. Husbands and wives in our society have affirming as a salient function, going beyond that of "support" in the economic sense and superseding "obey" (out of date) and "honor" (misunderstood) to include *espousing* the other's selves. Marriage, in other words, is between *persons,* in the theological sense, autonomous agents who recognize each other as moral equals, hence share, reflect, confirm the other in all good things. And the races and ethnic groups in this nation need to move to such recognition, in which the Other is no longer that antagonist and victim identified by the multiculturalists, but another form of the self.

This evening, I am alone in my dwelling with none but my cat for company, and I feel the solitude. Architecturally, not in a snobbish way, we are above the streets, looking out over the skies, neighboring buildings, gardens, and the bridges to the West Bank—as, from his island, Robinson Crusoe might have looked over the waves. Just out of sight is the high-rise, now a Ramada Inn, where Paul's mother lived until a week before her death; she too was alone, and for many years. Better to be lonely, though, than worse, as my Aunt Flora said; the price to be paid for companionship now would be too high. Anyhow, I do not expect others to fish me out from a solitude which is my doing as it is fate's. It is nothing compared to that of many others. There is a young chap I see often in the neighborhood, walking the neutral ground, standing on the corner of Louisiana and St. Charles, sometimes near the Columns Hotel, *always* without company, except what he gleans from others' presence in the streets. (People who see *me* walking up and down in old jeans, my mind clearly else-where—maybe on a poem—may suppose that I also am just another solitary eccentric.) He has some connection with Tulane, and I have seen him there also, loitering alone. He looks intelligent, but nature has not favored him: he is built like a string bean with a peculiar head on top. A yearning yet distant light is in his eyes. He reminds me of Carson McCullers's character in *The Heart Is a Lonely Hunter*. What can I do for him? Nothing. Nor can I help someone, a friend of sorts, who needs more than I can give: pretending otherwise would create ex-pectations that, when not fulfilled, would lead to a greater sense of abandon.

Such are the complexities of relationships on even a minute scale. Although the analogy between individual and community levels is imperfect, similar complexities obtain in society as a whole. As I wrote earlier, the fact that we can get along at all—given the human animal's aggressive instincts, the complexities of our developed brain, and sheer numbers—should perhaps astonish us. No better formula for wide-scale social and political har-mony has been devised, surely, than the Constitution of this nation, whose wise provisions, duly amended, can carry us far, if we do not forget to honor them. The courts should see to that, rather than engaging in social engineering that goes beyond statutes. Meanwhile, we could refuse racist rhetoric and extremist demands that offend common sense as well as political principle; we could require change from institutions (primarily schools) that presume to exceed their instructional mission, nar-rowly construed, to undertake remaking pupils' views on the family, sexuality, and marriage, and fill their brains with confusing, often deleterious sociological dogmas. Likewise, we could refuse the images of human relationships that commercial entertainment offers us. Televised domestic or "friendship" dramas and sitcoms are not only preposterous; they form viewers' ideas of how families are supposed to work, or not work, so that the dysfunctional family, a genuine and deplorable social phenomenon, has become amusing, even chic, along with absurdly demanding, invasive friendship, disloyal partnership, promiscuous sex, and an utterly amoral outlook. We could revive courtesy, the oil of human workings. And we could practice charity and fraternity, understood in a religious or a political sense, or both. Whatever the limitations and failures in defining and carrying out these principles in the past, cannot new efforts be made?

These prescriptions are scarcely original; little in this essay is. I am no Rousseau, no Hegel to devise new theories of community. But the views of Rousseau—that disputatious, maladjusted, paranoid genius—on society and its governance ultimately turn good sense on its head and invite tyranny; they were not unrelated to the Terror. Voltaire had a much better understanding of human behavior and what social organization could accomplish. As for Hegel, we know to what distorted and misguided uses his lofty theories were later put. Nor have I ventured here into more than a few angles in the maze of human transactions. What will that matter, if these observations have value as reminders or testimonials? Such is about all that moderate views can do. Those I consider disorderly, subversive, politically irresponsible (not to say blind), possibly incendiary—or simply misguided—but are strident, are heard continually, thanks to their own maneuvers and to journalists who, whether by strategy or simply uncritical acceptance, give them ample press. Now, as the bridge lamps begin to come on, first low, then gradually brighter—one span ahead of the other—and reach full illumination, hanging like Oriental gardens over the river, joining east and west banks, I imagine how words of courtesy, good sense, and reconciliation could shine on us all.

It has been now nearly fifty years since I lived year-round in that part of extreme West Texas that belongs to the Chihuahuan Desert, but my mind is connected to it still, as though magnetized by, or magnetizing, its strange mineral soils and the lodes of ore running along the Rio Grande and through the Chisos Mountains. When I was fifteen, my parents made the move mentioned earlier, to the Big Bend from Colorado—a new attempt by my father to escape the world that was too much with him. Did I appreciate the desert less when I was growing up in its light, surrounded by arid hills and pure skies, with miles of barren space literally outside the front door? Perhaps. "The true paradise," said Proust, "is the paradise one has lost." That we human beings cannot fathom our present fully is a poetic as well as a psychological observation; it is part of our makeup as beings by whom time exists. Heraclitus and Zeno noted ages ago the paradox of living in an instantaneous present that cannot be arrested, gone as soon as it arrives, represented by an arrow which, although apparently immobile at any single moment, nevertheless flies. "We look before and after / And pine for what is not /Our sincerest laughter / with some pain is fraught"—so wrote Shelley, the prince of feelings.

If I now see the desert differently, conceivably better, from the remove of an adult lifetime spent elsewhere, this is for three reasons. First, my vision as a girl preparing for the university was chiefly prospective, not circumspective or retrospective. The young must engage their energies and attentions in a forward direction, toward their potential selves, especially if they are fortunate enough to be healthy and vigorous, as I was. Second, the passage of time is a magic lantern, a set of optical lenses affording a range of visions over years and territories and beings of the past—visions more precise, more subtly illuminated than before, embracing both a nearly microscopic view, which pauses to count each tiny purple flower of desert verbena among the sage, and a cosmic view, in which all of Texas seems like a pinprick. Finally, my understanding of the desert has been heightened by the experience of living for decades below sea level in New Orleans, where the average annual rainfall, as last reported, is sixty-two inches. Immense trees take up most of the sky here; greenery pushes through fences and overflows the gardens; giant roots lift and split the sidewalks; and for half the year one can barely breathe, or so it seems. Confinement implies windows from which to look out. To use Proust's image, Noah never saw the world better than from his ark.

According to the *Columbia Encyclopedia*, the desert is an "arid region, usually partly covered by sand, having scanty vegetation or sometimes almost none, and capable of supporting only a limited and specially adapted animal population." By "arid" is meant an annual rainfall of ten inches or less. Vast parts of Texas, New Mexico, Arizona, Utah, and Nevada as well as some of California and Colorado meet that definition, though they have in many places an abundant growth of mesquite, greasewood, creosote bush, yucca, and cacti. For that matter, some of the Great Plains belonged originally, or still belong, to the category of middle-latitude deserts. Major Stephen H. Long, an explorer of the High Plains west to the Rocky Mountains, observed in 1821 to John C. Calhoun, then Monroe's secretary of war: "We do not hesitate in giving the opinion that [the area] is almost wholly unfit for cultivation, and of course uninhabitable by a people depending upon agriculture for their subsistence. . . . The scarcity of wood and water, almost uniformly prevalent, will prove an insuperable obstacle in the way of settling the country." In 1859 Horace Greeley spoke similarly of the desolate landscape of western Kansas and Nebraska and eastern Colorado— "the acme of barrenness." The Grand Valley (that is, the valley of the Colorado River on the Western Slope)— now laden with orchards and vineyards but once arid— illustrates how it is only by irrigation from wells or diverted river water that the desert, as Isaiah wrote, "shall rejoice, and blossom like the rose" (35:1).

Acquaintances sometimes say, when they learn I have driven through the Southwest, "What did you want to go out there for? There's nothing but desert." But what if that desert is myself?

As a girl, I was in touch with it by vision (cholla cactus, prickly pear, horizon rippling in waves of heat), sound (rustling of wind, chirping of cactus wrens), taste (dust in my mouth), feel (sand under my feet), smell (desiccation of summer, sweetness of blooming catclaw, scent of rain on dry earth). During my undergraduate and postgraduate years in muggy Houston and France, there were, in addition to visits home, long automobile treks across New Mexico, south to north, and into Colorado, then back south almost to the Rio Grande. One summer, we went by train across West Texas, southern New Mexico, and Arizona to Los Angeles, then returned from San Francisco through Nevada and Utah to Colorado before turning south again for Texas. These journeys provided a variety of desert landscapes: the desert mountains and high rangelands of south-central Colorado, the saguaro cactus forest of Arizona, the vast, uninhabited expanses of central Nevada, the white sands of New Mexico, the alkali flats east of El Paso, the folded mountains of the Big Bend.

The lasting hold over me of the desert and its rugged hills is confirmed by my collection of old postcards of the Big Bend—postcards of the smaller dimension no longer sold, some of them purchased from an eccentric couple, Mr. and Mrs. Theophilus, in their shop on Texas Highway 118: Judge Roy Bean's cabin at Langtry on the Rio Grande; Boquillas, upriver; Santa Elena Canyon; Mexico as seen from the U.S. side; the Chisos Mountains, including the Window in Big Bend National Park; Cathedral Mountain, Twin Peaks, and Paisano Peak in Brewster County; Mitre Peak and Indian Lodge in Jeff Davis County. I also have an extensive collection of postcards of the mind—mental images of sliding down the White Sands using trash-can lids as sleds; of hiking near Cloudcroft, New Mexico; of young Girl Scouts, with me as leader, climbing Mitre Peak.

The objects around me recall other desert landscapes and cultures. On a window ledge beside me as I write stands a photograph of the Organ Mountains east of Las Cruces, New Mexico. A small Navajo weaving adorns my desk; another covers an adjacent chair. A basket made by the Papago Indians in southern Arizona is both decorative and functional. Two pieces of Native American pottery, one (I think) from Santa Clara Pueblo, dating from the 1940s, and a more recent one from Cedar Mesa in Utah, keep me company. As I write this, I wear Navajo earrings, a Zuni bracelet, and turquoise beads from Santo Domingo Pueblo.

I helped bury my father in West Texas in the late 1960s. In the years that followed, it was wrenching to revisit the desert in which his eyes had found relief from melancholy, and to experience all over again the irremediable loss of one whose mind had animated the desert for me. I feared touching the strings of the desert's lyre; their note—that of the mournful wind whistling all alone, without reply, through the creosote bush and mesquite, over the ridges of glinting sand, over the random desolation of the stones—was an unbearable lament. Had it not been for my mother, it would have been, I thought, better not to go back at all. Then she too took her place in the arid earth. Thereafter, it seemed preferable to return even at the price of suffering, if this was the only way to see what their eyes had last rested upon. Surely the offering was due to those who had given me everything. So I drove and shed tears, trying not to be blinded by them along the highway. Later, without renouncing the debt, I found it possible to enjoy the desert even more fully, as an homage to them, and in so doing to reenact my past—as well, perhaps, as to rediscover something deep set in the human species. To reacquire the desert landscape, not by purchase of land but by contemplation, has been the business of many years since.

The sources and forms of any lifelong attraction are multiple; we are palimpsests on which both nature and anti-nature have written their lines. In the case of the desert, the light is paramount. It enables me, as Camus wrote, to "carry my lucidity to the end." It filled Marc Chagall with wonder when he visited the Near East in 1931. Georgia O'Keeffe and other painters who settled in Santa Fe or Taos valued its extraordinary effects. O'Keeffe's paintings of animal skulls depend on desert light to illuminate both life and death, to portray the misery and grandeur of existence in their proper proportions. Then there is the pull of space, to which, unless we suffer from agoraphobia, our gaze cannot help being attracted. What is the eye but a way of traveling beyond the body? A British friend who journeyed with me through the Southwest told me later, as she showed me the fine prospect over valleys and hills offered by her new house on the edge of Sheffield, that on that trip she had learned to value the restfulness of distant views. Emptiness calls forth its opposite, a sense of interior fullness that, unimpeded by ceilings and walls or natural obstacles, is free to expand.

Another appeal of the desert is spareness—*dénuement*—simplicity, economy, understatement. Spareness takes forms geographic, biological, moral, social, economic, liturgical, architectural, musical, literary, graphic. In religion, it is asceticism or at least simplicity, like that of the Shakers. In architecture, it can be a severe Romanesque chapel, marked by bare stones and a plain altar, or a Dutch Reformed church whose only adornment is light. In biology, it includes the desert's highly efficient animal forms, its miniature flowers, its larger plants with immense root systems and porous, water-saving fibers. In music, I think of Gregorian chants or the *Gymnopédies* of Eric Satie. In our lives, spareness is thrift; more broadly, it is connected to the impulse to flee machinery and large industrial complexes. There is in me something of the Luddite—not because my livelihood is threatened by mechanization, as that of the weavers was threatened by the mechanical looms, but from general moral principle, which tells me that it is unsound for either an individual or a society to enter into servitude to its products. "One believes one possesses," says Gide's Ménalque in *L'Immoraliste,* "and one is possessed."

Geographically, spareness often accompanies vastness: icy polar wastes, high peaks unrelieved by vegetation, endless desert sand. These spectacles have appealed to many, in part because of their very barrenness, even because of their aura of hostility and danger. While we human beings, who appear to have sprung from earlier species nurtured by the plentiful waters and luxuriant greenery of equatorial Africa, once needed natural bounty to feed us and caves and forests to protect us from heavy rain and searing sunlight, now, however, abundance can seem oppressive. Joan Didion speaks in *Play It As It Lays* of old people at a run-down spa between Death Valley and the Nevada state line who believe in the "restorative power of desolation." Jean Pélégri, a French-

Algerian writer, writes in *Ma mère l'Algérie* of "the apparently empty space of the desert" as intended for "thirst and prayer." In Gide's *Counterfeiters,* Olivier tells Edouard that he can imagine committing suicide after experiencing such happiness that it could not conceivably be repeated.

The impulse of exceptional individuals has often been to flee the assurances of home and seek wider horizons or more rigorous, perhaps purer lives. The struggle to survive, which Darwin saw as species-related, can become the search for challenge. Think of Roald Admundsen and Richard Byrd, of G. H. L. Mallory and Sir Edmund Hillary. Ease and routine are rejected by the less exceptional, too: look at those around us changing jobs, changing wives, changing children, changing addresses at age forty or fifty. This is not new; witness Lafcadio Hearn in Japan, Robert Louis Stevenson in the far Pacific, Paul Gauguin in Tahiti. Irving Howe observed: "In American literature the urge to break past the limits of the human condition manifests itself through images of space. . . . The urge to transcendence appears as stories of men who move away, past frontiers and borders, into the 'territory' or out to sea, in order to preserve their images of possibility." "To sea, to sea" or "To the desert, to the desert" cry those seeking to slough off the old man and find renewal, even—or especially—if it be through want. Who was it who said that it wasn't the discoveries of the explorers he envied, but their sufferings?

Not that I am a true ascetic: no hair shirts, thank you, no cold gruel. But human excess bothers me, and has bothered countless others who, according to the ways of their times, sought to withdraw to monastic cell, hermit's cave, or tower (Montaigne's wonderful retreat, Vigny's "ivory tower"). Here is where two meanings of *desert* join—a wild region, on the one hand, and an abandoned, solitary, or deserted location on the other. According to Littré's French dictionary, the first meaning preceded the second, which arose by extension. The desert is an antisociety. It was in the geographic desert of North Africa that early Christian hermits found solitude, the topography supporting their isolation and holiness.

An oasis means nothing without a desert to surround it. Nowhere is rain more valued than where it is scarce; it is by deprivation that a coming storm, or the promise of rain in a dark cloud over a distant ridge, acquires its deepest significance. My own mental desert has watering holes, clumps of desert walnut and mesquite, shady groves of cottonwoods along the dry riverbeds, pines at the higher elevations, rain in the afternoon (and, to be sure, campgrounds and motels). I confess that, during past moments of unhappiness, I have used the desert as a crutch. I have looked backward to it when I needed compensation for a difficult present. But my desert imaginings were less dangerous than strong drink, drugs, suicide, and crime; and they did honor to certain ideas and beings dear to me.

All this is terribly Romantic, with its assumption, as Byron put it in *Childe Harold*, that features of nature can be "a part / of me and of my soul, as I of them." Well, that's perfectly respectable, if one is to judge by the many literary and artistic products of the nineteenth and twentieth centuries that have been concerned with self-investigation, self-expression, self-projection—often, though not always, in connection with nature. Romanticism is older than that, anyhow, going back not just well before 1800 but further; Shakespeare and even Euripides have been called Romantic.

I look to culture to support my taste for nature; I want precedents, spiritual fellows. In Scripture and literature of the Christian era one finds uses of the desert so varied, so ancient, so repeated, as to warrant classing it as a central motif in the human *imaginaire*. My concordance to the Bible lists forty-five instances of the word (noun or adjective) as translating four Hebrew words, notably, in transliteration, *midbar*. This is in addition to its function as the equivalent of the Greek *erēmia* and *erēmos.* Then there is the even more frequent *wilderness,* for which there are two and a half columns of listings in small print (I leave the task of counting them to eyes younger than mine). It translates a number of Hebrew words, including *midbar,* as well as *erēmia* and *erēmos,* the latter recurring in all four Gospels as the place of John the Baptist's holy cry. Then there is the Hebrew word *tsiyyim,* meaning "inhabitants of dry places," translated "wild beasts of the desert."

Why did the seventeenth-century King James Version translators choose now *desert* or *desert place,* now *wilderness* as the equivalent of these Hebrew and Greek words? The English terms, as given in the *Oxford English Dictionary,* are close and somewhat overlapping, though not identical. A desert is "an uninhabited and unculti- vated tract of country; a wilderness; now *esp.* a desolate and barren region, waterless and treeless, with but scanty herbiage; *abstractly,* desert condition or desola- tion." A wilderness is a "wild or uncultivated land . . . region or tract of land; a waste or desolate region of any kind." One thing is certain: like Shakespeare (as in Macbeth's "the multitudinous seas incarnadine / making the green one red"), the translators appear to have rel- ished drawing on two linguistic sources. *Wilderness* has a fine Germanic ring to it, coming out of Middle English from Old English, and being akin to Middle High Ger- man and Middle Dutch *wildernisse. Desert,* by way of Middle English from Old French and ecclesiastical Latin and, before that, Latin *desertus* (past participle of *deserere,* "to sever connection with, abandon"), adds the contrast- ing Romanic note and offers etymological authority to the meaning "uninhabited."

The frequency of the terms in Scripture is no surprise, since the biblical lands consisted in part of infertile areas and lay adjacent to others. To the scribes, the desert was close at hand as a concrete reminder of historical and spiritual trial: suffering, atonement, redemption. The arid lands joining Africa to the Near East through the

Sinai Peninsula were the site of the Hebrew children's wanderings after they left Egypt. Prophets ("like the foxes of the deserts," according to Ezekiel 13:4) sought refuge in the wilderness or came out of it; the psalmist sang that he himself was like "an owl of the desert" (102:6); hermits and saints, including Anthony the Great and Jerome with his lion and his sacred texts, retired to its solitude; John the Baptist cried in his unmistakable voice from its depths; and, greatest of all, Christ repaired to its confines as preparation for His ministry and passion. The term *wilderness* is sometimes applied also to the profane and secular existence of this life, as opposed to heaven and the future life; in this application, it cannot represent a retreat from the world but instead (as in Bunyan's "the wilderness of this world") *is* that world, with all its snares.

A yellowed copy of *Bartlett's Familiar Quotations* (tenth edition) lists over a dozen occurrences of *desert* (adjective or noun) in the sense of wilderness or deserted (place). Two are from Scripture: Isaiah's phrase "the desert of the sea" (21:1) and the desert rejoicing, quoted earlier. Another is from Plutarch, who speaks of "sandy deserts full of wild beasts." The earliest quotation from English literature, from *Othello*, refers to "deserts idle" seen in travels (1.3); next, chronologically, is Milton's *Comus*, which speaks of "deserted wildernesses." Surely the word *desert* was used previously by British writers, but not in phrases that have become quotable and familiar. There follow in Bartlett's phrases by Pope, Gray (from the "Elegy"), and Byron (four citations, including "Oh that the desert were my dwelling-place" from *Childe Harold's Pilgrimage*). One also finds quotations from Thomas Hood and Tennyson. Missing, strangely, from Bartlett's is Edward FitzGerald's well-known line (from his translation of *The Rubiayat of Omar Khayyam*), a line my father often quoted with the rest of the quatrain, while looking out across the barren range, his arm around my mother's shoulder or waist:

A Book of Verses underneath the Bough,
A Jug of Wine, a Loaf of Bread—and Thou
Beside me singing in the Wilderness—
O, Wilderness were Paradise enow!

The *Shorter Oxford English Dictionary* provides citations from Pope and Dryden, including the latter's "desart World." Then there are a few allusions to *wilderness.* I do wonder how early British readers pictured the desert of Exodus, the wilderness of Saint John. Perhaps the moors and peat bogs assisted their imagination. Certainly they did not have *National Geographic* to furnish pictorial details. The question arises of whether they were better off in that respect: that is, is imagination enhanced or impeded by photographic evidence?

In French literature, the desert appears very early in hagiographic texts, such as the thirteenth-century poem by Rutebeuf on Sainte-Marie l'Egyptienne, who, according to legend, spent seventeen years in the wilds. There are, however, few oft-quoted uses of the word before the nineteenth century; France, covered with great forests in the Dark Ages, was later stripped of most of them but, even when they were cleared, had no vast barren expanses. At the end of Molière's *Misanthrope,* Alceste declares he will retire to the desert—that is, withdraw from society—rather than remain in the world, where, to survive, he must practice what he considers unacceptable compromise with the truth (white lies, bargaining, paying court). His announcement is not meant to evoke images of sands; only students learning French, not understanding that the word means simply "isolation," imagine Saharan dunes with one lone, misanthropic recluse. Much more striking (partly because of its four nasal vowels and alliteration of *d*), though without visual precision, is Jean Racine's beautiful line "Dans l'orient désert, quel devint mon ennui" from *Bérénice* ("Among the Eastern wilds, what ennui was mine"). The affective burden of the line and its desert setting are beautifully matched (the speaker, Antiochus, suffers from unrequited love). Still, I am not certain just what Racine had in mind. Did he visualize limitless wilderness, dunes, a treeless horizon? Or simply a deserted spot—emptied at least of the one who, to Antiochus, is all?

After 1800, the desert—in both senses—becomes a favored motif and theme in French literature and painting and remains so throughout the nineteenth century. This is owing to two or three factors at least. The first is the voyage to America of François-René de Chateaubriand, an aristocratic émigré during the Revolution, and two works that came out of the journey, *Atala* and *René*. These romances and their wild, primitive settings—including Louisiana and Niagara Falls—brought the American wilderness to France. That Chateaubriand had never seen most of what he described and that his details were hugely wrong (caribou, drunken bears swinging on vines over the river, and herds of wild buffalo along the banks of the Lower Mississippi, from which the Appalachian Mountains can be seen) made little difference, I suppose. The topos of the desert as a place for pure, innocent lives was supported, of course, by the topos of the noble savage, going back in French literature as far as Montaigne, but not at the literary forefront until the eighteenth century, and popularized chiefly by Rousseau. After Chateaubriand published *Atala,* Lamartine gave verse form to the Rousseauesque impulse to flee society and retreat into one's own desert—generally, for him, an isolated place in a setting of either serene, undisturbed countryside or wild natural features.

A second factor is the popularity of the Near East in French culture. Napoléon had begun the fashion with his expedition to Egypt. Later, the invasion of Algiers in the summer of 1830 and the subsequent seizure, gradual pacification, and colonization of the surrounding territory by the French offered to travelers extraordinary opportunities for stimulating the imagination. Throughout the nineteenth century, painters and writers—Eugène Delacroix,

Théophile Gautier, Gérard de Nerval, Gustave Flaubert and his friend Maxime du Camp, Horace Vernet, Eugène Fromentin, Guy de Maupassant, and many others—became tourists in North Africa and parts of the Near East. (Flaubert believed that he had been born to live there.) The sandy or rocky deserts that they encountered were described in their letters home and later appeared in poems, paintings, and narratives. Flaubert's *Temptation of Saint Anthony,* which shows the fourth-century Christian hermit on his desert mountaintop in Egypt, is a product of this Orientalist impulse, as is *Thaïs* by Anatole France, in which the heroine, converted by a proselytizing monk, renounces the flesh and goes into seclusion among the female hermits of the desert. Even Spain was annexed by the Romantics to the imaginary complex of the Near East, reinforcing the image of barren landscapes where the reflective European or the native could be alone with his thoughts or God or Allah. Gautier's poem "In deserto" compares explicitly Spain's sands and rocky *sierra* with the desert where Moses struck the stone to bring forth water. Later, such figures as Isabelle Eberhardt, "la Bonne Nomade," who, disguised as a man, lived among the Arabs and traveled widely in North Africa, and Father Charles Foucauld, called "the hermit of Tamanrasset," who ministered to the Tuaregs, drew further attention to the Algerian desert.

This major artistic trend in nineteenth-century France found new modes in the following century. In Algeria, a local literature appeared, continuing the strain of travel literature but this time in the voices of those, such as Louis Bertrand, who, though of European extraction, lived there and thus saw the desert and its inhabitants as aspects of the Self rather than as Other. (Ultimately, indigenous writers—Arab and Berber—themselves took up the task of evoking the North African desert.) Rarely has the desert been so beautifully presented in literature than in certain pages by Saint-Exupéry and Camus. In *Wind, Sand, and Stars,* the former speaks of the period when he and one or two other pilots worked in Spanish Morocco. "The desert for us? It was what was born in us. What we learned about ourselves." In one episode, he lands on a high plateau or mesa with sides too steep for scaling, where, he is convinced, no other human being has ever set foot. Then there is the moving account of his crash in the Libyan desert along with his mechanic Prévot, of their wanderings and sufferings and their rescue nearly five days later by Bedouins. In these pages, the desert serves as a test and touchstone of the fundamental human enterprise of survival. Camus similarly wrote about the desert that he knew: although he grew up in Algiers, he visited the South more than once and clearly assumed it personally as a kind of interior landscape, combining the opposites of poverty and riches, exile (a principal motif of his) and the kingdom. One need not be familiar with biblical parallels to understand his usages, but it helps. To his stories "The Guest" and "The Adulterous Woman," anyone who appreciates the American desert can respond immediately: the vast prospects, the ferocious winds, alternately hot and cold, the dunes, the empty sky.

The sky and the ocean, we know, often stand for freedom and possibility—the human dimension of potentiality, which the imagination projects onto these natural features and which they may in fact instrumentalize. The story of Icarus shows that men dreamt of flying for millennia before it became possible; Samuel Johnson picked up this desire in *Rasselas*; aviation writers such as Saint-Exupéry and Jules Roy wove into their narratives the connection between flying and personal freedom. In the early masterpieces set on the Aegean Sea, water supports a project (the Argonauts, the armada bound for Troy) or provides a test (Odysseus wandering over the waves). Those who fly small planes or practice hang gliding speak of the exhilarating sense of freedom afforded by moving through the air, as sailors feel freedom in the movement controlled by their hands at the tiller or on the ropes. (Larger vessels and jumbo jets may impart a similar sense to their captains and pilots, but I doubt it: everything is too mechanized, and the connection between human will and the response of the vessel is mediated by hundreds of tons of weight and thousands of wires. As for passengers, they may enjoy themselves, but the sense of conquering the elements is hardly the same on the *QE2* as on a small skiff gliding along in the wind.)

Mountains may also connote freedom, particularly the high mountains of the Romantics (as viewed by Childe Harold, for instance), which afford privacy, isolation, and expansion of spirit ("I will lift up mine eyes unto the hills"); but they often signify obstacle, even entrapment. Forests, jungles, and swamps are even less suggestive of freedom, though in fact those fleeing society, especially policing authorities, have often found shelter or eluded their pursuers there. Fairy tales are full of dark woods whose very mention chills the listener. As for gardens, their privacy—whether charged with religious overtones, as in the cloisters of monasteries and other houses of retreat; erotic connotations, as in *Le Roman de la Rose;* or simply horticultural delights—rarely signifies liberty. The walls or hedges suggest confinement, and one is alone there for only a while at best, with the eye of God or perhaps some spy or lecher looking through the shrubbery, or an ear listening behind a tree. (In the desert, you know who's at your back— likely, no one.) This is not to detract from the principle of "To Althea, from Prison": mind does indeed conquer matter and the human soul can, with only its own resources, find emancipation even within confinement.

Who would deny, upon seeing a photograph of figures on camelback outlined against undulating dunes or a red sky, that desert, like the sky, sea, and mountains, signifies not only trial but also the freedom to be oneself? In Camus's "Adulterous Woman," the heroine, looking out from the rooftops in the desert city that she is visiting with her husband, sees in the starry abundance and limitless sands the image of a human potentiality and fulfillment of being that she has never before experienced. Even the nomads, glimpsed in the distance in their camps, seem to represent liberty, as she imagines that they go where they wish to go, sufficient unto themselves, following no marked route. (The very real difficulty of their lives does not invalidate her feeling.)

The wonderful thing about the desert is that visually and imaginatively it is so close to the other geographic correlatives of freedom. Unless there is a dust storm, the desert provides views of the sky unbroken by lines of trees or other interfering vegetation, not to mention warehouses and skyscrapers. In the daytime, the desert sky is a pristine blue, since the air is not hazy with humidity or city dirt; at night, it is so laden with stars that one thinks they can't all possibly hold on up there and must come plummeting down. The desert's vast horizons similarly remind us of the ocean; here indeed are waves, in the form of dunes. This is not merely *my* imagination. Shakespeare offers the description "Environed with a wilderness of sea," and Pope the line "To roam the howling desart of the main."

True, I am not really sailing, or flying through the sky, as I gaze out over a desert landscape and the celestial dome above it like a royal baldachin, but the eye sails and flies. Then, if I wish to look at mountains as an extension of this dream, I can scale, mentally, a distant ridge and a farther chain of arid peaks, or—if I am in the extreme northwest corner of New Mexico—Shiprock, the great basaltic monument that, before the Spanish came, the Native Americans, knowing nothing of sailing vessels, called the Rock with Wings. The Arabs and other inhabitants of the deserts of Africa and the Near East used "ships of the desert": dromedaries or camels. I can travel over and around these nearly marine vistas and climb the mountains (some of them, at least) in my Jeep Cherokee, whose powerful engine and big tires might have been envied by Mercury the messenger.

What moments my own ship of the desert has let me

collect! I think of camping with my Colorado cousins at Bottomless Lakes, Navajo Lake, Chaco Canyon, all in New Mexico; Lake Ganado, Canyon de Chelly, and Monument Valley in Arizona; the Canyonlands area of Utah. I relive the splendid two-week camping trip I took in 1998 through New Mexico and the deserts of the other Four Corners states with my British friend, mentioned earlier, and her husband, who had traded the gorse and bracken of the Yorkshire moors for Mormon tea and juniper. In particular, the feeling comes back of our first night, beneath the shade of a fine pecan tree watered from wells, with our tents well stabilized against the hot desert wind, wine in our cups, and chili simmering on the fire. From those days and nights in the desert and its adjoining mountains, luminous moments still shine in my memory in pure western colors: white from the heat of noontide sun and dazzling gypsum dunes; gold and amber from endless sands and long rays of sun; turquoise and deep lapis lazuli from the sky; dusty blue-green from the sage; dark green from distant forests; black from obsidian and basalt and the nighttime desert sky, whose piercing stars only deepen the darkness. And just now I have returned from a long sentimental journey, like all such travels a bit Proustian, over much of the same territory, seen this time in the light of autumn rather than high summer, with dust storms, heavy rains, hail, and, in the higher elevations, snow covering the stones and arroyos, making the rough places plain.

During this journey, while I was visiting my cousin Edith in western Colorado, she asked me why, now that I am no longer engaged by Tulane University, I simply don't leave the soggy climes of New Orleans for southwestern Colorado, where I could live among sagebrush and piñon pine, and drive in a day or less to sites and landscapes I love: the mesquite-and-cactus rangelands of central New Mexico, the Great Sand Dunes, Monument Valley, Canyonlands, the Anasazi sites of Hovenweep, Taos. The reader may wonder also. While there are practical reasons (ties, duties, the proximity of a scholarly library where I know how to find things and can use the collections I've helped build), perhaps the most important reason is the least tangible. It is better, I think, to leave unrealized at least one founding dream, to miss and yearn for something—not the impossible, however, but the possible, the real, where the heart takes up its abode while the rest of the body fulfills its necessary commitments in a world of work. Mesas shine most brilliantly from afar. In my mind, they glow now, at first dawn, shadowed red and shaped fantastically like the figments of night; then taking on precision of outline, becoming dark-green tablelands under turquoise skies; whitened later by the blanching sun of noontide; and finally, at sunset, deeply colored with the riches of the day—crimson, burnished gold, low purple, burning across the sky, then shading into darkness, *largo, largo, pianissimo,* falling into sleep.

Of the various ways of going back to my native Colorado, I had not expected to indulge in this one: a brief visit (of the "gust of wind" type) in winter to Aspen, the playground of the rich, the celebrated, the glamorous. Indeed, I have railed against such places and the people who fly into them in private jets, build large, often unseemly houses, expect codes and laws concerning land and water usage to be bent for them, drive up prices, create road congestion, and help change the character of a mountain village, turning it into an outpost of Miami Beach or Southern California chic. Except for a stay in Winter Park long ago, some weekends at the Homestead in Virginia, and a brief drive through Breckenridge, I have generally avoided ski resorts and watering places frequented by the famous. Yet here I am, in mid-March, in the very heart of this playground, and by my own will. It certainly suggests that my position on the matter was not very firm. Put more favorably, it demonstrates how flexible I really am.

It all began through a neighbor, a young woman of style who is familiar with Aspen, Vail, Palm Beach, Beverly Hills. Reporting to me about her Christmas vacation in Aspen, she then spoke about the fashionable activity there in March, particularly the famous "Sneaker

Ball," given each year by Al Gross—the point of which is to show off evening clothes and the most original sneakers one can find or create, and, more subtly, to go so that others will know that you have gone, both those present and those so unfortunate as to be without tickets, to whom it can be reported. Some weeks thereafter, she proposed that I accompany her and a friend; her contacts are such that she would have no trouble, even at that rather late date, in obtaining tickets to the ball and guest privileges at her club, as well as arranging for rooms. Another acquaintance—an older man—might join us.

I did not yield immediately; temptation takes a little while before it works on me, usually by means of my imagination. A cockeyed idea, I told myself, to go flying off to Aspen, which I might not like, spending huge sums of money (by the standard of my weekly disbursements at home), quite likely encountering ghastly weather, perhaps being snowed in, yawning and teary-eyed with boredom. But I had been working much too hard during the previous weeks, more or less tied to my desk by the strong ties of compulsion, involving things I *must* do, to meet deadlines, and others I *wished* to do. "Alternate rest and labor long endureth," saith the proverb. A trip to Colorado would at least loosen the chains, if not afford, strictly speaking, rest. The change in scenery would be refreshing; do I not love the mountains, from which I am separated most of the year? "Come where mountains beckon / Pine and aspen grow," urges the song "Romany Road." The peaks were already starting to take on shape and coloration in my mind. The invitation was gracious, furthermore; I should feel flattered. It would be fitting to accept. Why not? My schedule could be rearranged to accommodate a few days away. I resolved only not to get a new dress for the ball—everything I have would be new to Aspen anyway—and to keep the sneaker cost down, if possible.

We left New Orleans on Thursday, the four of us—my neighbor, whom I shall call Karen, her charming friend from Florida, Suzanne, and the fourth member of the party, to be known here as David, to protect his identity. He was once—perhaps still is, if some are to be believed—a member of a profession recognized by its distinctive garb as well as its way of life. But I understand that he has put off the garments of this calling; certainly he is without them now, and he seems to be trying very hard to reintegrate himself into a world from which he had distanced himself earlier. Perhaps, however, it is harder to be mundane than people believe. Mufti does not quite suit him, and his attempt at a fashionable hair style, a bit long, produces only the effect of straws sticking out on an old broom. Later, I will have occasion to mention the Hemingway-Fitzgerald exchange on "the rich are different from us," observing that I am on the side of Hemingway ("Yes, they have more money"), but David's own behavior suggests that Fitzgerald's essentialism may not be without merit. Certainly, he remains thin-lipped, his brow permanently knit as if in puzzlement or censure, and small talk does not come easily to him. Dropping names—all the way to that of President George H. W. Bush, whom he met at a conference and shook hands with, despite disapproval of his politics—is one means he uses to contribute to the conversation. Nodding knowingly and solemnly at everything one says, even before the words are out, is another. Can he really anticipate everything? I think not; I have read a *few* things that he has not, and our views differ not a little. Lest, however, I seem mean-spirited, lacking in the charity that his creed holds to be the greatest virtue, I shall add that he is courteous, willing, cooperative—altogether quite a good sport.

It must be specified that, from the beginning, I informed Karen that I did not intend to ski. Though born in these parts, I nevertheless did not take up that sport as a girl, for practical reasons, and have seen no need as an adult to do so. The money to be spent on equipment and routine travel to the mountains, the time getting to and up the slopes—perhaps lying supine in bed, recovering from an accident—I prefer to spend in other ways. Besides, being a bit acrophobic, I am not crazy about swaying cable cars, and chair lifts even less. Terra firma for me, thank you. This is not to blame others' skiing. To my way of thinking, time—even leisure time—is to be used *well*, not in mindless or mind- or body-degrading pursuits, but in recreation—*re-creation*—suited to the person. If skiing restores the spirit of its aficionados, so much the better. Walking in town in their gear, with fish-eye goggles and sweatbands like karate artists, wearing heavy anoraks that make them look upholstered, and with rigid plastic boots colored purple, yellow, turquoise, or hot pink, they are as ungainly as moonwalkers, if more colorful, and like them bounce along in an unearthly gait. But they look happy. Anyhow, there is no obligation on me to ski; our arrangement is like that of the Abbey of Thélème in Rabelais's *Gargantua,* where the motto is "Fays ce que voudras" ("Do what thou wilst"). And when, candidly, I say that I have come to Aspen to *party* (keeping quiet about my desire to gaze at the peaks around me), everyone understands. My three companions, who likewise wish to party, nevertheless have stated their intention to try the slopes also, although in fact when the visit is over they will not have done so, venturing out into the snow only by means of a snowmobile excursion.

After our flight from New Orleans through Dallas to the Eagle County Regional Airport, a lengthy drive by van awaits us, and night has fallen when we arrive finally at the hotel. It is a mediocre establishment, the lobby, restaurant, and bar tacky, my room ordinary, dreadfully overheated, without remedy, since the thermostat does not work, and too close for my taste to the noise of whirlpool bath, pool, and pool tables. Yet since by resort standards it is a bargain—about one-sixth of what the top-of-the-line costs—I would not think of complaining. After arrival, the girls (I can call them that—they are younger than my own daughter, and as a woman I cannot be accused of sexism) take an hour or so to repair the travel damage and make themselves even more beautiful than they were, while David and I leave almost immediately for the St. Regis Hotel next door, which has a lovely bar and lounge, where we order wine and a hearty soup. (He has stopped to put rubbers over his shoes, given that some snow is piled in the streets. It is the first time in years that I have seen those half-galoshes; can one still buy them or has he saved them from his youth?) The crowd at the St. Regis is well dressed, a trio is playing, and there is dancing—real dancing, not disco ersatz. David observes, "This could become addictive." A physician friend of mine who goes skiing in Colorado often has reminded me about the effects of alcohol at eight thousand feet; and I recall how my cousin Beth's husband, when having to deal in his official capacity with woodenheaded, obstructionist, legalistic bureaucrats from an agency in Washington, who knew and cared much less about Colorado than he, sometimes conveniently forgot to tell them that drinking too many martinis at high altitudes was unwise. So, for now, one glass of wine is the limit.

After a while, Karen and Suzanne come to meet us, and we go off to the new Club Chelsea, associated with its homonym in Vail, both run by a friendly woman named Judy. The front room, with a few tables and two musicians, is packed, as are both the bar area and the smoking room, whose fauna is visible through the glass partition, as in an aquarium. To be crowded is the mark of an establishment's success, and half of Aspen seems to be here. Karen, obviously one of the cognoscenti of Aspen life, leads us toward the bar; we order, shouting above the din, and, a soda water with lime in hand, I lean back to watch and listen, like that minor character in Proust's *Swann in Love* who, upon being asked what he is doing at a party, says, adjusting his exophthalmic monocle in his eye and rolling his *r*, "J'observe!"

Something for which I am scarcely prepared occurs shortly. I must explain that Karen, not herself a member of the literati, nevertheless is a tremendous booster of my work; she is the closest thing to a publicity agent I have ever had, beyond the publisher's staff. She even wants me to write an epic novel on Colorado, the sort that Hollywood might buy. As bodies move back and forth at the bar, in tidal surges, she snags a few and introduces me as the author of *The Shimmering Maya*. Now, although that volume was reviewed very favorably in the *New York Times Book Review*, it was scarcely a best-seller; it was not directed toward consumers of popular culture, even the superficially sophisticated (more like sophistic, or sophomoric) culture of Aspen. But this evening, at least two people so addressed smile and say, "Oh, yes." A hundred-to-one that they have never heard of either the book or me. A third person tells me she liked it a great deal, and a fourth asks (neutral position) how it is selling. No one will acknowledge ignorance. When, the next day, a man asks me what I write, I answer, "Poetry, essays, criticism." The first two appear to hold little meaning for him, to judge by his countenance; he does not even *understand* the third term.

My reaction to Karen's campaign is unease; there is, I feel, some misrepresentation in all this, words not really meaning what they appear to mean—although everything she says is in fact true. But it would be impossible to explain to listeners that perhaps they mistake that book for another, that I am *not* a celebrity, but rather chiefly a poet and, even in prose, a writer for the happy few (to use Stendhal's term, borrowed from Shakespeare's *Henry V*). The next evening, the same thing will occur. When Karen explains who I am, a fellow feigns knowledge and inquires with interest whether the book's sales have "peaked." Here we witness a type of seriality achieved through advertising: Karen, a self-appointed publicist with great charm and a convincing manner, has turned me (momentarily) into a commodity with which one is supposed to be familiar, and those within earshot will not admit to not knowing my work. For the time being, I am a product of their imagination.

After watching further the ebb and flow of people, I decide it is time to turn in and walk back to my room, leaving the others to stay until Chelsea's closes. Friday morning, I am awakened at an hour of the hotel's choosing by the cacophonous modern music of a vacuum cleaner. Declining to patronize the breakfast room, I look for a coffeehouse. It is then time for a long walk, under what turn out to be perfect skies and mild temperatures; my British tweed jacket soon becomes a bit too warm. What I see in this brilliant sunshine is reassuring: many buildings left from the 1880s and 1890s—the time my grandparents on both sides arrived in Colorado or a decade or so after—the corbels, cornices, pediments, and quoins intact, the bricks a warm red or yellow, the turned or sawn gingerbread freshly painted, largely in pastels. In turn, I visit St. Mary's Church (date unknown to me, but turn of the century, I should think); the Pitkin County Courthouse, a small monument in its side garden to the dead of the Vietnam War; the Red Onion, once a renowned house of pleasure; and the Hotel Jerome and Wheeler Opera House, both now restored, originally built by Jerome Wheeler, who, like a goodly number of others, amassed a huge fortune—millions and millions in silver—before repeal of the Sherman Silver Purchase Act in 1893 made the price plunge. The hotel bar, a massive construction in dark and ornately carved wood, with crystal ornamentation, is a finer version of those, then unrestored, that I saw with my parents in the 1940s in mining towns such as Central City, Silverton, and Telluride. I prowl around some small Victorian cottages, which are so like those in which my mother and aunts lived in Colorado Springs, and houses that my great-uncle John Hawley built, that I cannot suppress hot tears over all that nevermore will be and a stabbing pain at the thought of my mother's beautiful young womanhood, turned by time's crabbed hand into age, infirmity, and death. The sun is so bright that a hat would be nice—and all I have brought to Aspen is a wool beret, in case of extreme cold. Of the scores of fashionable shops (or so it seems), none appears to have just quite what I want in headgear. But here is a thrift shop, and on a bust near the door sits a fine black hat of western design, with small silver conches on the band, "Made in Texas, USA." The rest of the day, my eyes are well shaded.

Karen has given me instructions for the late afternoon: whatever she and the others may be doing, I am to go to the Little Nell bar at four o'clock to get a table for the *après-ski* gathering; they will join me. An elegant hotel at the foot of Aspen Mountain, adjacent to the ski-lift station, the Little Nell is where the crème de la crème gathers after the last ski run. Unfortunately, the place is packed already; all I can do is hold some standing room. I wonder how my companions will find me in this crush. But they do—principally, I suppose, because when Karen enters a room the men (more numerous here than women, and all rather predatory), drawn by her exotic beauty, move toward her and open a channel, like seas parting. While I practice reserve, few others do. It is like a club, where no one is a stranger; first names are the rule, last names being given only if there is some particular reason to do so (as when someone points out another person from New Orleans, and upon the exchange of full names, I discover that he went to school with Paul). A woman later comes up to David (he will report), tells him she has a backache, and inquires whether he would like to give her a massage. No need to bait one's hook and hope for a strike: the fish jump into the boat. Another woman tells a tall fellow in western dress, "I like your hat and your boots." "What about the man in between?" he replies. A fellow touches my arm, points to Karen, and asks, "How many drinks has she had?" When I reply that a woman should tell neither her age nor what she has drunk, he is not deterred; a quick maneuver, and he is beside her and summarily fills her glass, conveniently empty, from a champagne bottle he brandishes.

After a prolonged cocktail hour at the Little Nell, it is time to dress for the rest of the evening. Having changed, we meet again in the hotel lobby and start out for Piñon's Restaurant, reputedly the finest in the town. There is a long wait; *Le Tout Aspen* favors this place. In fact, fancy food of the very refined and pretentious variety is mostly wasted on me—for instance, the *haute cuisine* at the Restaurant Lasserre in Paris, to which a friend invited me once, and at which I appreciated only the cold asparagus and a sorbet. (I like to *recognize* what I eat.) The featured Colorado dishes (elk, buffalo, rack of lamb, large steaks, pheasant, trout) are not unappealing, but all of that will be either too rich for me, hard to cut, or full of bones; I choose salmon with leeks, regretting it then, for the preparation is not what I would have preferred. Oh, for a simple plate of *spaghetti al pomodoro* with a salad, or red beans and rice, or a Mexican dinner.

We then go to the Caribou Club, to which Karen has entry. Neal Travis called this internationally known establishment of Harley Baldwin "the best private club in America." Surely it must be one of the most crowded; Chelsea's appears, in retrospect, quite airy next to the smoke- and noise-filled rooms of the Caribou. Disco music screams through the place, and flashing strobe lights approximate a visual variety of Chinese water-drip torture. The women, with deep *décolletés* and evening sandals or high-heeled boots, and draped predominantly in expensive black materials such as leather and velvet, are generally elegant but resemble plastic dolls. I note an extraordinary palazzo-pants outfit in brocade, the side of the trousers slit all the way to the hip. Evidence of money is everywhere. If I taught and wrote for five hundred years, I would not have what this young real-estate baron to whom I have just been introduced has recently made—some $300 million. There *is* a problem: what does one do with all that money? Literally, sometimes, the rich probably do not know. Unless it is to be dissipated, it must be managed, invested, watched. My own ethics would require that I exercise a vigilant custodianship of such a fortune, as of any more modest one—a dreadful responsibility, which the gods have spared me.

Again, I return to the hotel by myself; it is late by my measure. Tomorrow evening I must be in fine form for the *pièce de résistance* of this adventure, the Sneaker Ball. Walking up the hill to the hotel, I am greeted by another woman, doing the same. She is elegant in her ankle-length fur coat, but we both have high heels and find the going difficult in the brick-paved pedestrian areas. "Sneakers will be wonderful tomorrow after this," she volunteers, adding, "Men don't know how lucky they are, with their loafers." She then launches onto related matters. "Look at what we do for them! After we've had our nails filed and polished, our hair streaked and set, our eyebrows plucked, and a bikini wax, they *should* pay for the evening!" Perhaps the fur is part of the payment.

The oven-atmosphere of the hotel room and noise around the whirlpool bath, even at that advanced hour, make rest difficult, but finally the body takes over and finds its way through the tunnel of darkness into sleep. The next morning, I again go to the coffeehouse, chatting over coffee, juice, and muffin with two lawyers from Washington, D.C. I can see why they would wish to leave for a while that place with its numerous and widespread scandals, from the sleaziest sex behavior in the White House on President Clinton's part, with a creature lacking all qualifications except *embonpoint* and its equivalent in hair, through investigations or indictments of a half-dozen cabinet members and financial corruption involving illegal contacts with quite scrutable and obviously very dishonest Orientals. Breakfast over, I again have the better part of a day at my disposal. Another walk is in order, this time to study more recent architecture and enjoy the way in which most of it (not *all*, alas) echoes and blends very well with the older styles. It is pleasing to see how many solar cells have been installed. I admire the fine draft horses hitched to carriages, awaiting clients for a slow tour of the town; they are the animal equivalent of the high-horsepower pickups, Jeeps, and other heavy-duty vehicles that predominate here. There are many fine dogs around also, all well behaved. A bit more shopping follows, during which I note very few southwestern items for sale: we are north of the line that separates the territory explored by Frenchmen, where such terms as *butte, coulée,* and *plateau* are common, from that settled by the Spanish— the *mesa* and *arroyo* lands. I also browse in the art galleries, which are quite fine. Here is a pleasing metallic sculpture, of mid-size, in a stylized totem-pole design; but neither my baggage nor my budget can accommodate it.

Time then for a classic American hamburger. I know I am in the West: when I ask the waitress to cut the mayonnaise, she assures me that the house *never* puts mayonnaise on hamburgers. After lunch, I find a seat in the sun near the skating rink and, peeling off scarf and gloves but protected by my hat, I work for a while on some translations I have brought along. Just before me are the steep slopes of the mountains, whose trees, stony outcroppings, avalanche lines, and ski runs offer pleasing contrasts of white, dark green, and silver. Above the crests, the sky, as hard and brilliant as blue topaz, holds a few paragliders in Crayola colors; their drifting movements are like those slow, circular currents of thought that bring into waking reflection the fluidity of dream.

We have agreed to meet again at Little Nell's, and this time I arrive well before four to get a good place on the sun porch. Before the others join me, a fellow asks to sit down; I invite him to do so on the condition that space be left for my friends. He is a developer, a breed that generally puts me off. What he has to say is, however, rather encouraging. He claims concern for limiting growth, conserving resources, preserving styles, and building midcost housing (partially underwritten by the town of Aspen) for service personnel, integrated into neighborhoods of more expensive structures; and his seriousness is borne out by the large amount of information he shares with me, and his apparent sensitivity about the land he owns, the mines and miners, water and mineral rights, and other aspects, past and present, of the complex relationship between human beings and nature in this territory. Yet in his struggles with the county commissioners over some planned land use, I might be on their side . . .

By this time, Karen and Suzanne have arrived with their usual entourage of swains, who sometimes come and go, as in a ballet, but mostly stay. One is said to be related to the Windsors; perhaps, for at least he has an educated British accent. Another fellow is introduced as Sir Henry Something; I wonder whether he was knighted for telling dirty jokes, as he is now. A man from Akron sits down with us after a while. He seems quite fascinated by Suzanne. A manufacturer (he says) of sophisticated wheelchairs for paraplegics, he is nevertheless a perfect jackass. (Great oafs from Akrons grow . . .) Telling in one alcoholic breath about his young children, and how much he wants them to stay out of trouble, in the next he speaks with animation about seeing strip shows on Bourbon Street in New Orleans. He inquires what I do; I give him my card. The letters *Ph.D.* puzzle him; I explain. He then supposes I am a philosopher. "Good for you!" he proclaims. (I have not waited on his approval.) "God bless you!" I reply that I hope He will indeed, since, to judge by what is around me, my worldly blessings have so far been modest.

The girls eventually pull themselves away from their admirers and return to the hotel for a two- or three-hour preparation for the Sneaker Ball. They will skip dinner, having, like David, eaten a late lunch as part of the snowmobiling excursion. Since I am hungry and it will take me only twenty minutes or so to get dressed later, I go off looking for a Mexican restaurant. La Cantina, on Main Street, has been recommended, and rightly so. With a large margarita in hand—the altitude adjustment having been made—I order a plateful that turns out to be copious. Halfway through the meal, a server comes around to ask whether I have finished. Good heavens, no; he will get a fork through the hand, I explain with a smile, if he tries to take the plate. When he next comes around, it is entirely empty. "My Lord!" he says, "you ate *all that?*" What can I do but explain that I have had a great deal of experience at eating Mexican food.

Some while later, I am ready for the ball, waiting in the lobby. David joins me. The girls report by telephone that they are still dressing. So we two go off to the St. Regis, where the ball will be held, with plans for them to join us eventually. In the bar, a trio is again playing; the trumpeter doubles as a singer, doing New Orleans jazz numbers. This is the *avant-party* preceding the ball, which then will be followed by the *après-party.* The occasion is suited to a favorite occupation of mine in odd moments, studying footgear and its wearers. Those who have tickets to the ball are easily distinguished from those who do not, and the accounterment of the former—tuxedo or dress suit, slinky cocktail dress or ball gown, combined with various styles of running shoes and sneakers—makes for delightful watching. My own modest sneakers, of canvas, with pineapples printed all over them, make a fetching combination with my rhinestone earrings and floor-length black knit dress. David has new ankle-high athletic shoes with outsized tongues, combined with a tuxedo and an old lined windbreaker as a coat.

I study the crowd. There are lots of young men with

beautiful young women, and older men with beautiful young women. The latter are almost uniformly slim, not to say anorexic; *one* woman has a tummy that sticks out a bit. Neither here nor at the ball will I see anyone visibly pregnant. Do these men not want heirs? Of course, some already have heirs, from wives they have left behind. I note a handsome gray-haired fellow in his fifties accompanied by a striking and exquisitely coiffed young woman whose short black dress displays shapely legs; her natural attributes have been enhanced, I believe, by a product made by the Dow-Corning Company.

On a love seat near our chairs sits a man of some years, dressed in what looks like a raccoon coat, sneakers, and a western-style hat. (The old stricture against men wearing hats or caps indoors has disappeared, obviously, save in some pockets of good manners; half of the male youth of this nation sport baseball caps indoors and out. When Bum Phillips was coach of the New Orleans Saints, he never wore his trademark Stetson in the Superdome, having been taught by his mama, he said, to uncover his head indoors.) The fellow inquires of David and me whether we have tickets to the ball; despite his sneakers, he does not. We answer yes. He offers to buy them off of us. I reply that it would be most ungracious of me to sell mine, since it was a gift; David agrees. Later, I shall wonder what the fellow would have offered; it is rumored that scalpers are getting as much as $1,000, but I doubt that. He asks whether we cannot help him get in . . . using contacts, perhaps. He also inquires about the status of David and me: "Are you together? Are you married, or an *item?*" Now this creates a tricky moment. While not wishing to embarrass David or offend him by making it clear that he and I *never* will be an item, I do have to indicate that we are together only casually. So I reply in a matter-of-fact tone that we are acquaintances, members of a small group from New Orleans.

Encouraged, perhaps, the raccoon-coat man comes

around to my left side. He asks my name, including last name. "Brosman with an *s*, or Bronfman?" I explain. "Do you know who the Bronfmans are?" Perhaps not entirely by chance, I can identify them as the Seagram's gin and whisky people—adding (with a complacency that may be ungracious but which he brings out in me) that, while they have a colossal fortune, I am wealthy in the ways of the mind. "May I ask you a personal question?" I reply that he may ask but I don't have to answer. In fact, it is not very personal. "Do you believe in love at first sight?" "No," I reply firmly. Is this his usual line?

He is not deterred. "May I ask another?" This one is of a different sort. Touching my silver locks, he says, "Why don't you do something about that hair?" (He means dye it, of course.) Will my readers understand that if I were a man (well, of course, then he wouldn't ask), those would be fighting words? Women, I have always believed (and many agree with me, though perhaps not the woman in the long fur coat, or others here), are not objects to be made over for men's pleasure; they are absolute, not relative, beings, and should retain their autonomy of choice in the way they see and shape themselves. Even if we seek to please, we must first please ourselves. So the fellow gets an answer that sounds a bit impertinent but is really very pertinent. "This is *my* hair and I'm not changing it for you or anyone." I explain that I am *what I have done,* not what hairdressers can make me. The poor fellow does not understand; he cannot "read" me, being used to a different sort of woman. In a gesture of reconciliation, perhaps, he removes his hat and gestures to his mostly bald head. "That's the hair I've got." I must forgive him. Doing so is made easier by his perspicacious comment in our next exchange. He asks if I have children. I tell him that I have one daughter, a real sweetheart, who lives in New York and is married to a fine man. "I have three," he counters, "and I like two of them—a pretty good average."

The Sneaker Ball itself, to which we gain access by giving up our tickets and displaying our shoes, is, as you might imagine, an anticlimax. The purpose is to *go*; there is little, really, to do. The entranceway and cloakroom are indescribably crowded. Sixteen hundred tickets were distributed to the host's "closest friends," we learn (I guess the raccoon-coat man isn't one of them); perhaps some fourteen hundred people are present. In the main room, a cash bar is set up, dispensing watery drinks in plastic cups; a few nuts remain in a bowl in which innumerable hands have dipped. Fortunately, there is an ice-water bar also, at which I help myself repeatedly. In the adjoining room, a band plays at many decibels; disco lights flash, and gyrating is going on. Even if I wished to join, it would be hard to break through the crush, as tight as the Saints's defensive line. The corridor leading to the restrooms has become an auxiliary party, men and women separating by sex and gathering near their respective doors. At least there is enough room to breathe a bit and examine sneakers. My favorite are a pair of red Reeboks, decorated with lace and false jewels and flashing lights. Another woman has put baby sneakers over her ankles, like bracelets, with dress shoes on her feet. Among the men's, I like best the gray tennis shoes to which the tops of snakeskin cowboy boots have been affixed.

Karen, gorgeous in a black dress with spaghetti straps and high-heeled, sequined sneakers, finds us and leads us to meet a friend or so. One fellow introduces himself to me as Jack. He claims he knows the entire family of hosts; do I? He comments on my stance—elbow on hip. "Aggressive," he announces, but adding, "I like that." I explain that it is not offensive but defensive—a bumper position, an attempt to ward off attacks, like that of a man who a moment ago simply walked into me. (Experience at Mardi Gras proves useful; I just stood there and made him back up and go around.) In less than two minutes, Jack has remarked that we are of the same generation (not so—he is distinctly older) and that he can still make love whenever he wants. Had I inquired? Certainly not.

Finally, all this is depressing; waiting in a crush like that of a rowdy football crowd in England, I get my coat and leave. Two major religions, to one or the other of which many of these people ostensibly subscribe, proclaim that "Thou shalt not covet." Alas, there has been much coveting here—and more in the past, which made some of this wealth possible. It is plain, moreover, that the divorce between money and culture is almost complete. While the old English class system was founded on many injustices, and was the source of innumerable economical and moral ills, it had the merit of holding wealth in the hands of those who, broadly speaking (with numerous exceptions, of course), had some taste and knowledge: they bought books and read, collected art, supported the theater, poets, and musicians, traveled to the Continent, paid for public monuments and other works, and built and maintained splendid houses and gardens, along with concerning themselves with civil government. Few members of the class were quite without instruction, and many had great learning; its accumulation and transmission benefited society as a whole. At present, the wisdom of the ages is nearly lost even among those who could afford to acquire and appreciate it; neither philosophy, nor literature, nor history beyond that of recent years has much meaning for them. (Art and music are different: one can show off one's art collections to impress guests and be seen by others at the opera and symphony concerts.) While the human spirit is a *given*, a fine soul must be nurtured, cultivated; culture is its food as well as its product.

Outside, the mountains that ring Aspen and the Roaring Fork Valley stand like Swiss guards, tall and majestic, cloaked in black velvet, their halberds raised and peaked helmets outlined against the sky; the sparkling tiara of a firmament studded with stars crowns all.

This land once belonged to others. Here and there, small ranches remain from the turn of the century; eastward across the Continental Divide, buffalo and Plains Indians once had dominion; and in all the surrounding territory, Utes lived up until the second half of the 1800s, along with mountain sheep, antelope, deer, and other game in large numbers. Through movements of population, military action, political policy, and economic development, the settlers and their governments either devalued or destroyed these undertakings and resources, or took them over, causing displacements and even decimation of earlier dwellers and vast herds. Those displaced people were sometimes similarly cruel, as well as extremely primitive; we should not romanticize or idealize them. Moreover, a clash of cultures such as the one I sketch here and thousands of others that have taken place—of which we are all the more-or-less distant products—is bound to favor the more intellectually and technically advanced. Put differently, the Indians were a conquered people—like countless others, from small tribes to vast nations, in the course of human history, the world around. One deplores, nevertheless, the brutality of many acts, the destruction of valuable traditions and resources, the wholesale indifference of the exploiters. O brave new world! Was it for the Sneaker Ball and the Caribou Club that the buffalo died, the Indians were removed?

Sunday is devoted to an easy morning, then an afternoon tour (for David and me—the girls are recovering from their late night) of the environs, with a very pleasant and knowledgeable driver. The tour is advertised as appealing to those who like *People* magazine, *Entertainment Tonight,* and *Architectural Digest.* I tell the driver, "I like only one of those—you can guess which." I also stress my interest in nature, landscape, history, and geology; David says he is of the same mind. She points out striking examples of recent domestic architecture, adapted more or less well to the environs; I admire the use of logs and river stones but find certain of the houses obscenely enormous. The protected areas and some structures remaining from the nineteenth or early twentieth century and the spectacular drive up Independence Pass to where it is blocked for the winter compensate only somewhat.

We then meet Karen and Suzanne at the hotel and are off to a private party, given by George Scott of New York, at Club Chelsea. It is a "Lick Your Wounds" party, the wounds being those of the Sneaker Ball. Of course it is crowded, but we find places near the bar and order, taking advantage too of some guacamole dip. Karen makes her rounds, then disappears. It turns out that she has gone into the smoking room, which resembles somewhat the snug of a British pub; we follow. None of us smokes, but there is more *gemütlichkeit* here than elsewhere. The purported Windsor is present, along with a number of other Brits, who doubtless like the atmosphere. One is named Byers. When I tell him that a peak above the Fraser Valley to the northeast bears his name, he smiles in delight. A deep sofa cradles a middle-aged Englishman and a blond woman, quite charming, of Dallas and Atlanta, whose accent is to his as melted butter to crisp carrot sticks. They have met this very day, it turns out, but are already the picture of love; Cupid, like alcohol, works very fast at this altitude. George Scott himself is there, in a red silk brocade smoking jacket. I thank him for the invitation, procured through Karen, of course; similarly, I have spoken to the host of the Sneaker Ball, recovering at the bar, although he hasn't the least idea who I am.

Dinner takes place in a Japanese restaurant: the four of us, plus an elegant friend of Karen's from Beverly Hills and two charming, courteous Brits. We must wait a long time (I think only the intervention of the Californian gets us a table); champagne for all, meanwhile. I do not care for Japanese food, nor can I use chopsticks well, but it would be unseemly not to go along with the band.

A fork is provided, happily. By the close of the meal, I am weary; the vacuum cleaner played again this morning. Am I the only one of this group who needs sleep? And we must be up early to catch the van, which will return us to the tarmac at Eagle County Airport. The others elect, however, to finish the night in a club somewhere. How they will get up I do not know. Suzanne must fly back all the way to Tampa, and this coming weekend Karen will leave for Hollywood to attend the Academy Awards ceremony. They, at least, are young. For a few days, I have been so with them.

Tomorrow morning, during the drive through Glenwood Canyon—whose multihued and dramatic beauty has been enhanced by patches of snow that the winter sun has left in the shadows, like a chiaroscuro painter—and later in the confining capsule of the plane, I shall meditate on all this. Pleasure in the right dose is good, certainly, even the disorder of pleasure. Dionysus was a god, and Christ himself provided wine for the marriage at Cana. Both the Greek and the Christian tradition, in addition to the cult of Mithra, the great Egyptian cult of Osiris, and certain others of which we have knowledge, feature, according to textual, oral, or graphic evidence, ritualized banquets and orgies of diverse sorts—moments given to fellowship (or "bonding"), to sharing of solemn mysteries, to enlightenment, to dispossession of the rational self—but often involving purification and penance either before or after, and sometimes preceded or followed by sacrifice and death. What forms my post-symposium penance will take remains to be seen. Whatever transpires, at the cocktail hour, if I desire, I can imagine the sounds of liquid jazz flowing warmly through the St. Regis bar, and feel the crush of limbs and trunks in the dense and alcoholic forest of the Little Nell; and in my midnight mind, the sharp nocturnal outlines of the Aspen peaks will shape themselves against the starry firmament of thought.

Writing in 1933 about one of his most famous poems, "The Cemetery by the Sea," Valéry spoke of "these very imperious verbal illuminations which impose [on one], suddenly, a certain combination of words—as if such a group possessed some intrinsic force." He noted that the poem was "at first only an empty rhythmic figure, or filled with empty syllables, which came to obsess me for some time." He then described the steps by which the rhythm came to dictate the rest of the poem's composition, including a pattern of contrasts and correspondences. Most significantly, for my purposes, he discovered that such a pattern demanded that the poem be "a monologue of the self, in which the simplest and most constant themes of my intellectual and affective life were called forth, woven, and placed in opposition, as they had imposed themselves on my adolescence and become associated with the sea and the light of a certain spot on the shores of the Mediterranean."

What interests me in these reflections is the connection Valéry establishes between an "empty rhythmic figure," a "verbal illumination," occurring for no visible reason, and the exploration of the self, carried out in this case in metaphoric terms within the poem's system of images, but self-exploration nonetheless. That a particular word pattern would always lead to such self-examination I would not claim. But I agree with Valéry that a nearly preverbal or verbal pattern of sound *may* be tied to a corresponding feeling about the self. A similar view has been expressed by the American poet Stanley Kunitz, who writes: "Language itself is a kind of resistance to the pure flow of self. The solution is to become one's language. You cannot write a poem until you hit upon its rhythm. That rhythm not only belongs to the subject matter, it belongs to your interior world, and the moment they link up there's a quantum leap of energy. You can ride on that rhythm, it will take you somewhere strange." Valéry observes, it should be noted, that the themes of his affective life became *opposed* in the poem, the rhythm leading to identification and then interweaving of contrary impulses. Although the logic of this step is obscure, it seems appropriate that rhythm, which is, after all, a combination of contrasting beats, appears connected so immediately in the poet's experience to an intimate monologue that is really an exchange involving multiple, contrasting themes of the self. As much as any other explanation, certainly, Valéry's analysis sheds light on the stages by which an obscure aesthetic intention or feeling can develop into a complex verbal construct.

The reader will note that I have passed here, surreptitiously, from the genesis of a *poem* to that of creative work in general. It is my view that certain other forms of writing, among them the autobiographical essay, can spring from sources akin to those of poetry, develop somewhat similarly, and achieve like effects. While this position would be rejected by any generic purists who may remain—those who would argue for a radical distinction, in aesthetic theory and practice, between poetry and more discursive genres—it is defensible, I believe. Certainly in my own case, as both poet and autobiographical writer, I can vouch for close connections between the genres.

This is so first of all because almost any writing that is

not intended only to impart information can be, or be appropriately made, "poetic" in some senses—utilizing indirection rather than direction, figurative language such as metaphor, personification, and symbol rather than blunt statement; painting verbal images; expressing the aura around things rather than just the things themselves; calling attention to itself *qua* language. This is so likewise, and more profoundly, because the writing of one's life can be seen as a creative act—what some would call the construction of the self. This written self is first of all, to be sure, a function of the *lived* experience prior to, and during, the writing, not merely a literary invention; and this lived experience is, in turn, a three-way synthesis of the givens of one's birth, the situation and circumstances of one's development, and the intervention of one's choices, or freedom. But—to return to my claim that the autobiographer is creator as well as recorder—if we agree that the self is not wholly determined from birth but is rather an evolving process and product of living, we can assert also that the autobiographer's enterprise adds a fourth dimension, that of self-interpretation, which combines past experience with present reenactment through memory, to create, in the mode of language, the fullest self the author can grasp. Belief that autobiography is nearly consubstantial with the self is not confined to the modern, subjective age, in which the Romantic identification of subjective experience with truth continues to hold great sway. When, in the preface to his *Essais,* Montaigne wrote that he was himself the subject of his book, he implied—and all his writing implies—that the book was himself: he had constructed himself in writing. Similarly, Pepys's motto, "Each man's mind is his very self," suggests that if ways of thinking are integral to the personality, ways of writing are also.

Now certain principles at work in self-writing and their effects seem loosely similar to those that operate in music, as suggested by the vocabulary that can serve for both: rhythm, and, to a lesser degree, color (a painter's term suited to the work of certain composers, such as Debussy), tone, mood (a psychological term), harmony, perhaps harmonics—terms that Valéry uses in connection with style—and, obviously, themes, a basic aspect of both arts, thematic recurrence and pattern being among the most fundamental features of literary writing and most easily assimilable to music, from Bach's *Musical Offering* and Mozart's *Magic Flute,* through nineteenth- and twentieth-century programmatic and operatic music, to jazz. My challenge is to demonstrate that these terms are indeed suitable for autobiographical texts, where their verbal equivalents create decorative values for the inner eye and ear, appeal to our desire for variety within recurrence, participate in the structuring of the work, contribute to a pleasing sense of wholeness, and produce effects in the reader.

Because one does not ordinarily read prose aloud, there is of course no real auditory experience; even aloud, prose has no regular beat or system of sound repetitions. (In verse, when recited, usually only the meter and end-rhymes are noticeable; and to them, as to other sounds, it is extremely risky in my view to attribute inherent meaning—one vowel being more "cheerful" than another, one consonant "feminine," and so forth.) Hence, in prose the musical terms I propose are figurative. But the reader's inner ear is sensitive to unheard sounds, transmitted through printed words, and punctuation and other visual clues, added to the words and their images and associations, can be evocative, inviting to revery and creating linguistic "music." This holds for much expository writing—even discussions of ideas, as the prose of numerous philosophers shows. How this is so will be considered shortly.

For the moment, I should like to digress to talk about music as such, or rather, about my tastes; although personal, this ramble will make a general point. Up to the mid-nineteenth century, and in most cases well beyond,

Occidental music was very formal and structured, and that's how I like it. Prior to the Romantic period, strict forms were the rule, from sixteenth-century madrigals to late-Baroque fugues, cantatas, concerti grossi, and the developing symphony and concerto, although over the centuries there was also enormous evolution in genres and styles. The beat was firm, the key stable or modulated only in fixed ways, and chords were built according to rules. One knew what to expect; the very form of the piece, plus the melodic, harmonic, and contrapuntal material on which each was built, and the standard patterns of recurrence and variation, allowed listeners to anticipate the flow of the rest. This formalism did not mean that no emotion was communicated. Much of Bach and Handel is highly charged music; and what works are more profoundly moving than Mozart's last symphonies, or his D-minor piano concerto?

A loosening of form with the Romantics and post-Romantics, along with a different understanding of the manner and matter of music, led to emphasis on theme over structure, and finally in the twentieth century to compositions such as those of Olivier Messiaen (who, I read, "avoided regular rhythmic patterns by altering the duration of his notes by fractional amounts [and thus] hoped to express the idea of timeless eternity") and the later works of Arnold Schoenberg, whose musical rationale and form are said to exist but escape me completely. This is surely a shortcoming or obstinacy on my part, but past remedy, since my parents did not play such music for me in my childhood and I have thus not interiorized its patterns, unlike those of Mozart and so forth, which take up all available room in my musical mind. (From this sweeping condemnation of modern music I do except numerous compositions by Debussy, Ravel, Poulenc, Vaughn Williams, and a few others.)

In contrast, in literature I am quite willing to deal with, and enjoy, looser forms, which characterize much modern writing, such as free verse, prose poems, and freely structured fiction. I positively *like* Proust's meandering, if subtly constructed masterpiece, in its seven principal parts and more than three thousand pages. But I believe there is more than taste involved here. What is it that makes notes into music rather than random, meaningless sounds? No note having meaning or even giving much pleasure by itself, music cannot rest on isolated, discrete sounds, or even on a few bars, but rather depends on sequence; one note or chord must lead into another and so on, until in some manner the listener is alerted that no more will follow, the development having reached its conclusion. To my way of thinking, the giving up of conventional structure and logic in most modern pieces has led to some very sappy, dissonant, and cacophonous stuff, the formal development of which is impossible to follow—and, at the extreme, to a random, meaningless world of sounds that fits perhaps the universe of post-Newtonian physics and the political chaos of the twentieth century.

Language, however, is different; it is symbolical, and words *do* have meaning, by definition—arbitrarily arrived at (except for onomatopoetic terms) but recognizable and agreed upon by members of a linguistic community. Moreover, because of this meaning adhering to verbal sounds and their arbitrary written equivalents, the mental processes involving them are different: one follows and remembers their *meaning,* synthetically, and recurrence is not crucial—there need be no fixed time signature, no repeated bars. In short, language, unlike music, is *cognitive.* The variety of words is greater than that of notes, their scope and combining power are immense, and, in prose at least, one looks for novelty, in so far as each sentence is expected to carry further the exposition, analysis, or narration. This allows for the construction of elaborate and lengthy verbal systems of immense variation, made up of smaller structural units, whose underlying logical, dramatic, or narrative structure is loose—like an immense polyp, or an island in the

Sargasso Sea—but comprehensible nonetheless. The classical epics are the prototype of such, although they followed strict metrical patterns; later, Chaucer, Rabelais, Montaigne, Shakespeare, and Milton created new types of such flexible structures, and European novelists have been doing it ever since Cervantes. In fact, until the experiments of the French New Novelists, the novel was almost universally a story or sequence, and thus chronology itself generally furnished an underlying structure, even if the composition was episodic. "Plot" was *what to expect.* Similarly, in the essay, various clues, including the title, the *incipit* or opening, and the tone, give a sense of what is to come, and in biography the basic pattern of life furnishes a fundamental structure. In short, for coherence in literature, one does not need rigid rules and forms. Freely organized verbal structures can be effective, up to the point where words approach a nearly random jumble, as in certain postmodernist texts.

This means—to edge back closer, finally, to my main points—that rhythms and other musical qualities in autobiographic prose are freer and more subtle than in music itself; yet they do exist and can be aesthetically effective on the scale of the whole work, and sometimes its constituent parts. These rhythms are the beats and tones of experience itself, of which I shall speak in a moment; and then the means by which these existential rhythms find expression in corresponding narrative patterns, which in turn create coherence and other types of aesthetic appeal.

The first means is style. "Style," writes James N. Stull in connection with autobiography, "is an epistemological strategy that both reveals and defines reality, a 'reality' . . . that is often a highly personal and metaphorical interpretation of material and social worlds. . . . It is . . . a testament of authorial selfhood . . . a way of creating a self and arresting experience in the moment of language by symbolically possessing the world." Style is the autobiographer's personal voice, with its rhythms of thought and speech, its distinctive blend of tones—although normally it does not reproduce verbatim actual speech, marked by colloquialisms, redundancy, undisciplined sentence structure, hesitations, disorganization, trailing off. The eighteenth-century French scientist Georges-Louis Buffon, asserting that "style is the man himself," defined it—in terms that apply to music also—as "the order and movement that one puts into one's thoughts." The rhetorical voice can be multiple, including the voice of the narrated self, to the degree that it can be separated and reconstructed by the narrating subject, and the voices of others who have been part of the subject's circle and who are present through quotation or paraphrased speech. One may also unconsciously incorporate elements from others' writing, or consciously adopt models and their tones and rhythms: no matter, if the rhythms become an integral part of the author's own style.

In this personal style, verbal equivalents of rhythm, tone, pitch, and color in music are found in the nuances of word choice; in the mixing of concrete and abstract language, familiar and learned expressions, personal and literary examples; in patterns of variation and recurrence, including various word-echoes such as alliteration; and in the characteristic shaping of sentences. English prose has obvious verbal cadences; ternary structures are highly favored, but binary rhythms may be more fundamental to autobiographic writing, for reasons to be suggested in due course. Other rhythms are constituted by contrasts in sentence length—the short sentences of three, four, or five words contrasting with those several lines long, containing numerous clauses and digressive elements. Emotional tone is established likewise through affective vocabulary—words of anger, regret, dismay, impatience, joy, serenity, whether on the part of the narrated subject or explicitly that of the narrating voice. Tone is a function also of the autobiographer's attitude toward readers—distant, superior, friendly, complicitous, and so forth. There are also the semantic resonances that a word, phrase, or image either acquires through its employ in the particular work or possesses already, owing to its conventional use by other authors; all writers draw on such charged verbal elements until they are rejected as utterly trite.

Certain words, phrases, and verbal rhythms seem affectively privileged, revealing writers' fundamental tendencies of thought and feeling, characteristic vision, inner music, and imaginary world. "Certain words sound in us," wrote Valéry, "among all others, like harmonics of our profound nature. . . . [They are] analogous to the universe of sounds, in which musical thought is born and moves." Like Valéry's spontaneous word pattern, they may be instrumental in dictating the development of personal prose—in establishing relationships and furnishing the structure of the whole. They may also tell more than does the autobiographical narrative proper—more, that is, about the subject's inner world and the way it has reacted with the surrounding milieu. In this very volume as well as in earlier essays, the word *desert,* a millenary *topos* in the literature of contemplation, has become invested with my own meanings, adhering to my particular experience and its moral and geographic context, so that when it is evoked, the reader "hears" mentally what has come before—vibrations, as it were, around the image.

As for structure, one can discern subtle rhythms at the level of composition in any extended narrative. A story built on a straightforward, rigid time line of single actions, each advancing the plot in a 1, 2, 3 sequence, would be not only tedious to read but short on understanding; whether one is recounting something from history, or a personal experience, or an invented story, a good narrative constantly breaks its basic thrust with rhetorical interventions, digressions, elaborations, and disruptions in the chronology that narratologists call analepses (going backward) and prolepses (going forward), as well as other variations such as acceleration, iteration, and ellipsis, and sometimes the important element of occultation—that is, *not* telling something crucial, whose absence is itself part of the story.

In short, there is in style and structure an existential element of *lived rhythm,* which often mirrors what I termed existential rhythms. True, one does not live one's life backward in fact, nor leap to the future, as the narrative can do, nor can one live "faster" at some times than others, in the strict sense. But inner life involves both anticipation and memory—something without which no self is imaginable; the film of mental processes includes flashbacks and flash-forwards, creating rhythm in the mind. The speed of experience likewise varies with circumstances and with age; weren't summers longer when you were a child? Moreover, emotional life is never uniform; it is a commonplace that joy follows sorrow in succession, discouragement elation, success failure, and these differences modify or "modulate" experience, creating rhythm, color, and tone. There are also fundamental biological and cultural rhythms: to the long-term rhythm of the organism, which has birth, growth, adulthood, and old age as its principal curve, unrepeated for the individual, although constantly recurrent on the scale of the species, are added the recurrent rhythms of bodily processes, the social rhythms of school, work, leisure, and so forth, the political and historical rhythms that mark culture either regularly or erratically, and, perhaps most significant of all, both obviously for life-forms themselves but also for human mythmaking, the rhythm of the cosmos and of the solar year, and all it has contributed to the imaginative life of the species.

Some of these rhythms, such as the movements of the stars, are highly regular and recognized by all; others are looser, but visible as one looks at a life as a whole. Moreover, there are idiosyncratic patterns in the life of individuals, which may be crucial to a person's development, particularly for the self-consciousness that goes with artistic endeavor, and central to the autobiographical project—the rhythms of illness and health, for instance (as in the case of Proust), or of travel, happiness and unhappiness, success and failure. Some writers identify what they take as ur-episodes, crucial events that, like a personal archetype, design a pattern for subsequent experience, whose recurrence is part of narrative rhythm. In connection with Mary McCarthy, who recounts such an archetypal incident in her childhood, one with religious import, Gordon O. Taylor speaks of her reenactment of her conflict through narrative, both as the persona's damnation and as "an emblem of salvation, with its own implications for the act of literary survival now being attempted in autobiography."

In addition to narrative rhythms that follow patterns of birth, growth, and decadence, autobiography is often organized around oppositions or dialogue, sometimes in oneself, sometimes between self and the world, concentrating alternately on one or the other, alike at the level of the recounted subject and the recounting voice, the latter responsible, of course, for everything else. The contrasts between inner and outer, self and others, contemplation and action, are fundamental in experience; even an introverted, solipsistic writer whose project has been to cut himself off from the world is obliged to deal with them—including at the moment of writing, since writing is in the world, not in him. Autobiographical texts tend in particular to alternate rhythmically between, on the one hand, reconstructed revery—that is, direct access to the putative inner self, or at least one of the selves—and, on the other, quasi-objective analysis, including considerations on the surroundings and events. The pattern created by such alternation is far from regular, and sometimes barely perceptible, but its absence would be noticed—not only because, for the autobiographer to emphasize the inner life without giving due notice to the outer, or vice versa, would strike readers as unbalanced, but because inner elements must needs have their echo or result in the outer world, and the latter inflect upon the former, at each stage of one's development.

Another alternating pattern involves dialogue *among* selves, often between the emotional self, on the one hand, and intellectual experience, on the other. The struggles between the rational life and the passions, particularly love or, in its most instinctual form, sexuality, constitute the heart of many autobiographies, as of much fiction. One form of this conflict is the confrontation of the child and the adult he inevitably, and sometimes regretfully, carries within him. Elsewhere, it is the drama between soul and body, that is, the pull of instinct or sin; any writer who adopts a theological framework in which to evaluate his experience will certainly have recourse to such a dualism, and many, such as McCarthy, do so even after they have discarded all theological grounding.

A variation on the struggle between emotion and rationality has both an individual and a cultural aspect: the opposition between romanticism and classicism. Irving Babbitt argued that all children and all women were romantic: classicism was the mode of the adult, rational (hence male) mind, and of such cultures as had reached and maintained control over the raw givens of the primitive human being. (It is curious to note in this assertion, which will strike many readers now as an irresponsible generalization or an abhorrent patriarchal statement, the same dichotomy established by the radical feminist Peggy McIntosh, according to whom men think "vertically," that is, logically, and women think "laterally.") Many autobiographies reflect the co-presence of these modes of thought and feeling, either as a simple opposition of childhood to adulthood, viewed respectively as romantic and classical, or as a recurring rhythm, whereby the subject is drawn now to the one, now to the other, then back. I will add one more opposition, unique to women autobiographers, and illustrated particularly well by Beauvoir in her memoirs: the consciousness of oneself as female in contrast to consciousness of oneself as a generic human being.

The antitheses I have identified, which constitute easily recognizable dyads, are complemented by the major dualism of past versus present, which underlies the entire autobiographic project. Whatever the author's technical choices about how to narrate a life, the present is a point of reference, usually an explicit one, conveying or denying meaning to what is recounted, or receiving meaning from it, since the past, to which it is opposed, is nevertheless seen on a chronological trajectory leading to the present, although the trajectory may be recounted through analepses and other techniques of interruption. One may ask in this connection whether autobiography is dialectical in the Hegelian sense. I shall answer that question later. I do not mean to suggest for now that all rhythmic patterns in autobiographic prose are neatly dyadic, although the archetypes of innocence and experience, sin and redemption, body and soul, night and day often can be sensed behind them, producing or at least fitting those binary sentences spoken of earlier.

Autobiographical projects are built usually also on a number of themes, sometimes explicit, straightforward, and linear, such as an artist's vocation carried out or the course of a public career, sometimes covert, circular, erratic; whether the patterns are strict or loose, they create narrative rhythm. Other types of recurrence and variation likewise create rhythm. Characters may reappear, in no particular order but in such a way that, like a leitmotiv in some music, they evoke what has gone before; and key words, repeated motifs, and recurring allusions create a fabric of self-reference, or autotextuality, just as in music—Beethoven's Fifth, for instance—a rhythmic pattern recurs from movement to movement.

A word, parenthetically, about parenthetical elements and what Jorge Semprun calls "concerted disorder." I do not identify an apparently digressive style with lack of mental rigor; in personal writing at least, one is not obliged to follow only one line of thought at a time or to use tight structures such as syllogisms. A mind digresses constantly, refining and adding to thought. Parenthetical additions and asides can afford a closer look at a topic, or a different perspective—the equivalent of walking around a three-dimensional object, or blowing up a photograph, or, in musical terms, variations on a theme. Moreover, like digressions in general, they may express the self more candidly than the outer frame of the paragraph and its ostensible direction. And—this is my main point—they contribute to tone and rhythm in an expected pattern of interruptions.

Testifying to the role of recurring patterns in autobiography, in a quasi-musical structure, Vladimir Nabokov wrote, "The following of such thematic designs through one's life should be, I think, the true purpose of autobiography." This stylized, even "musical," construct is, of course, an artificial one; all literature is artifice, as is music, even the spontaneous outburst of song. Does this imply aestheticization of human existence, perhaps at the expense of living? And does an autobiography that relies markedly on a thematic structure and other compositional rhythms distort the life story and approach the status of fiction? I said earlier that autobiography is a construction of the self. Socrates' dictum reversed—"The unlived life is not worth examining"—serves to underline that it is *life* that counts first of all. But the poetic making of autobiography is not to be confused with fabrication. In connection with his war experiences (he was interned in Buchenwald), Semprun asserted that only those who made of their testimony an artistic object, a "creation," could arrive at its "transparent density." More generally, invention of the self is not false and unauthentic, but is, properly understood, a different form of the process of self-realization through inner and outer choices, in which every human being engages through the mysterious processes of perception, imagination, reasoning, reflection, decision making, and other acts that compose the personality. And such self-creation has, both in the present of writing and the past of reflection, its own truth. Rather than *creation* of the self, perhaps one should speak of *subjective reality* and *coming into awareness* through language. The poet Jean-Claude Renard put it searchingly when he spoke of imagination's role in the "transmutation of being and the beginning of its accomplishment."

This does not mean that autobiographies cannot contain errors, misrepresentations, or other forms of falsehood, due to deliberate choice to mislead or to auto-misrepresentation—*of* and *to* the self. As James M. Cox observes, "Some writers make more than they record, since the making may be all the record they have; others record more than they make. No autobiographer can avoid doing both." Joan Didion and Mary McCarthy, among others, have spoken of the inevitable storytelling involved in memory and the resistance of "stubborn facts on record." Cox agrees: "Memory and all the motives involved in it sway the writer toward illusion and delusion." In memoirs by public figures or in autobiographies whose principal concern is the record of acts and circumstances, misrepresentation is potentially a serious flaw. But in the sort of poetic autobiography where "musical" values would be most significant—that is, where the drama is chiefly a subjective one and language is charged above all with rendering the inner rhythms of experience and feeling—"error" no longer has the same meaning. "Illusions," if given a role to play in the fabric of the autobiography and the pattern that emerges, are part of the narrated and/or narrating self; they thus have aesthetic justification at least. As George Gusdorf has put it, even when autobiography dissimulates, "there is a truth affirmed beyond the fraudulent itinerary and chronology, a truth of the man, images of himself and the world."

Deconstructionists such as Jacques Derrida and Paul de Man, who, relying on supposed insights from sociology, psychology, and linguistics, have exposed the self as a fiction, invite readers to remove the "subject" from autobiography and see the work as wholly an invention— something constructed by language alone, having no grounding in any knowable reality. All that remains is a pseudo-subject, "spoken" more than "speaking," created by the very language it purports to use. If one were to take these critics at their word, it would make little difference whether one called autobiography "truth" or invention, history or aesthetic object, since these theorists question the referentiality of language to the degree that determining meaning becomes impossible (except that of *their* texts, of course). The unknowability of the subject is paralleled by the unsayability of anything, and one ends up with either a primal scream of powerlessness or a generalized silence or asphasia like that of certain dramatic characters of Beckett and Eugène Ionesco. To restate the matter, such criticism has no business dealing with the particular generic traits of autobiography, since it has renounced its own capacities to do anything but accuse, pointing to the artificiality of any mental or literary construct.

For my part, I do not despair either of meaning, which E. D. Hirsch Jr. defended eloquently thirty-five years ago as stable, reproducible, and determinate, or of the subjective reality I mentioned above as it is explored and developed in autobiography. The way this reality becomes developed through self-writing allows me to connect the autobiographical enterprise with morality. To do so, I need to look briefly at awareness, which is of two sorts: the pre-reflexive consciousness, which is constant—a sort of ongoing humming of the self to which one need pay no attention—and the reflexive consciousness—a deliberate act of reflection, even a perspective taken on the self. The second, which is almost as continuous as the first, relies on visual and auditory images, both perceived and imagined, but also tends toward verbalization; it is the interior monologue that each person carries on most of the time. Its language is, however, rough—an uneven stream of elliptic mental enunciations, redundant, broken off, taken up again, corrected, abandoned—sufficient for the daily operations of living and a rudimentary self-knowledge, but rarely more. It is only when the language of the self is exteriorized, and chiefly when it is shaped into a formal construct—poem, autobiography, autobiographical drama or novel—that the possibilities for self-knowledge are enhanced well beyond the level of the quotidian. "Style," writes Herbert Leibowitz in this connection, "mediates between fact and the interpretation of fact." As Gusdorf puts it, autobiographical writing "is a second reading of experience, and it is truer than the first because it adds to experience itself, consciousness of it." And knowledge of self and self-in-the-world—the very topic of autobiographical writing—is certainly one of the grounds for moral reflection. Although I do not mean to imply hereby that morality is only an ego-centered, subjective choice, I am persuaded that authentic moral reflection needs the shaping, judgment, and scrutiny of experience to which an autobiographical project invites.

It will appear that I have abandoned my topic, autobiography and music. But the concerns just noted for self-scrutiny through writing lead me back to the question of dyadic rhythms, which are multiplied by the process of self-examination, since, to the opposing themes of self and world noted earlier, it may add the antithesis of error and truth, sins of the past and grace or redemption of the present, or past glory versus present decadence. The past as lived by the *narrated* subject is contrasted with that as judged by the *narrating* subject. Given that the text is linear—that is, written and read in time, and building as it goes along on its own "past"—these oppositions, which all have their own resonance, may lead, as the autobiographical project develops, to *new* corrections and insights. Thus the movement is not only contrasting but dialectical. Absolute closure and synthesis of life can come, of course, only with the subject's death, but anticipating that is the synthesis of the ever-deeper retrospective glance, with what I assume as its growing moral complexity. The rhythm of experience, with all its contraries and changing tones, is ultimately a triad: past life, present retrospection and introspection, and the synthesis of self that emerges in the writing. As Nabokov wrote, "The supreme achievement of memory . . . is the masterly use it makes of innate harmonies when gathering to its fold the suspended and wandering tonalities of the past." While music has a strong physiological basis, it nevertheless tends to transcendence, as song both expresses the root, visceral experiences of joy, triumph, and grief, and goes beyond them, forming and transforming them. One is tempted to say that, with its fluvial flow, its sonorities, its rhythms, music is more than a metaphor for human experience: at its fullest and best, human life *is* music, the acting out of rhythm and grace that allows the embodied, earthbound animal to leap over its situation. Perhaps—to change the musical metaphor slightly—one can imagine autobiography as a triadic chord, the past as root or tonic, the present as third, the fifth being the memory and the synthesizing mind, grasping the whole in a satisfying, harmonic shape.

ometimes, even before the summer's end, when the sun still gets up early, heating to white by noon, and the languid afternoons just mosey along, one feels the melancholy of measurement: June has once more gone out like a tide; time is notching again the yardstick of months and seasons and shortening one's future prospect. But even during dog days, the summer is still its possibilities, or rather, *our* possibilities, and reminds us in its own mode of a fundamental question, "What will you do with time?" Again, Texas and points farther west have magnetized my thoughts; I *intend* them, as the phenomenologists would say, and it is time to go back, retracing, with variations, a Texas journey recounted earlier in this volume.

An acquaintance of mine observed recently that he had just visited two countries new to him, Texas and Mexico. A new Texas highway map says, "Welcome to a country where the natives are friendly [yes] and the language barrier is easily overcome" (that depends on the visitor and the speaker). Is Texas really a different land? This question implies others: what role do geography, tradition, and the past play in our lives? what is the actual, and what is the proper, relationship (both political and other) between one of the fifty states and the geographic and political whole to which it belongs? what is culture? The place of the individual or other component within a larger collectivity remains one of the most fundamental and crucial questions in all political science and philosophy. To say that at the end of the twentieth century and the beginning of the twenty-first it imposes itself with extreme urgency is not to ignore, but rather to call attention to, the wisdom of those who dealt with the topic in classical Athens or those French, British, and American political thinkers of more than two hundred years ago whose enlightened understanding made possible a republic on this continent and a new departure in European politics. The concern has always been central to American political and social thought. But the questions of rights and responsibilities of individuals and groups and of the value of discrete cultural elements, having received new formulations and being affected by technological matters with far-reaching consequences, appear more urgent even than before, at both the national and international level. Do we want to be a new Yugoslavia? I shall meditate on these matters as I drive west, observing, listening, knowing the land again by direct contact.

The beginnings are the same: the drive from New Orleans to Houston, where I will stay with Evelyn Payne, a college friend, well read in literature and many other fields, whose loyalty has meant much to me. I shall lunch with other friends and have the pleasure of dining with one of my students, originally from Morocco, now finishing her dissertation and living in a Houston suburb, where she maintains a culinary tradition half North African, half French, and endeavors to cultivate a North African garden. Most of my friends here are, however, Texans. Evelyn comes from an old Texas family, established around Smithville well before the Civil War and connected to a large and important clan. This background is not unrelated, perhaps, to her conservative temper and convictions—although upbringing and tradition do not and should not necessarily produce their like, and those are legion who, coming from similar roots, have taken the opposite position, denying radically most of what their forebears believed and practiced. She is aware, as we all must be, of the clash of forces that have made our history, recent and remote. She acknowledges, for instance, that her ancestors owned slaves—but considers significant the fact that the latter all chose to remain on the estate after emancipation. Her great-grandfather, she reports, killed many Indians, but is quoted as saying on his deathbed that he had felt no pleasure in doing so and that he had deemed killing necessary in order to protect the women and children of the settlement.

Radical cultural critics would point out, of course, that the whites should not have been in Texas to start with: the New World was stolen from the natives, first by the Spanish conquistadors, then by the Anglos (who are accused of despoiling in turn the Hispanics and are often considered worse than their olive-skinned predecessors, white being the most despicable pigmentation). Critics of such simple mind (or bad faith) refuse to acknowledge that before the Europeans came, indigenous tribes had often invaded others' lands, tried to exterminate rival groups, sold captives into slavery, and practiced other barbarities, just as in Africa intertribal warfare existed long before whites arrived, and numerous peoples and chiefs engaged in slave trading against other Africans. (Nor shall I dwell on the more recent examples of tribal slaughter in Rwanda and Sierra Leone.) In short, while the Europeans in America had superior means and often numbers, conquest and oppression have not been confined to recent centuries or practiced only by those of European descent, and butchery and slavery are deplorable at any time. As for the aforementioned critics, they, like all of us, are products of violent encounters of peoples, clans, and cultures.

Moreover, I do not observe many of these commentators attempting to return to some ur-homeland in order to separate themselves from the nefarious political and technological products of recent history and the benefits of white oppression. Where would they find such a homeland anyway? What used to be called "underdeveloped" countries are frantically attempting to reach Western standards. (An exception, culturally speaking, though not economically, is Saudi Arabia. Shall we women all wear the veil?) In fact, the naysayers I have in mind all partake of the Caucasian culture by using electricity, driving automobiles, and so forth; with the exception of certain Native American critics, they live on land procured through the whites' presence in America, and use products from the industrial complex. Some would like to return this land, or its usufruct, to descendants of the *original* inhabitants; they are wise who will identify them. Meanwhile, are they prepared to have the same policy applied throughout the world? Where, then, shall we find the Canaanites?

Despite the pleasure at seeing generous friends, my appreciation of Houston is not wholehearted. (I hope not to offend by this judgment my gracious hosts. In fact, many Houstonians themselves rant against the urban sprawl that characterizes their city.) It is overgrown, too spread out, and too freeway-dependent, as I observed earlier in this volume; the center does not hold well, and neighborhood identity and cohesion can be found only in patches; the top-heavy and ill-designed new houses of the latest *nouveaux riches* are often vulgar in appearance, matching perhaps their owners; in short, the city lacks proper character, or at least what *I* take as character. (Perhaps I have been spoiled by living in New Orleans.) But, the parallels with Los Angeles notwithstanding, it *is* Texas, though not *my* Texas: the accent is right, things are big and dynamic, there is tremendous pride, a certain relaxed quality can be sensed, and people are not surprised by a good twangy "you all."

Next is the genuinely southwestern city of San Antonio, where, in foundrylike heat, the American Association of Teachers of French will hold its annual meeting this year—a concession to many members from west of the Mississippi. En route I pass through Waller County, not far from the ranch of someone whose life was once closely associated with mine, and of whom I think wistfully. Reaching downtown San Antonio and the hotel (the old St. Anthony, where my grandfather stayed in the early 1930s) and wearing driving clothes—jeans, a faded chambray shirt, and Bass sandals—I learn that an AATF reception is about to take place, at which various officials, including the French consul and the president of the Alliance Française, will be prominent; I am urged to attend. My garb is certainly not appropriate, but since there is not time enough to change, I agree to go as I am. It turns out that I will not be the most casually outfitted—a few people lining up at the ballroom are wearing shorts—and I have on my turquoise necklace, bracelets, and earrings, proclaiming, to westerners at least, that I am dressed up. I am reminded of a heavily bejeweled woman whom my cousin Beth met, along with other officials' wives, at a convention of western electric power-company representatives in El Paso. During a conversation about house burglaries, the woman was asked whether she didn't fear her jewels would be stolen during her absence. Following Diamond Jim Brady's principle ("Them that has 'em wears 'em"), she answered, "Oh no, honey, all I've got is turquoise and diamonds and I always wear them all." (Some years later, her husband was led away in handcuffs, accused of misappropriating corporate funds; perhaps she has had to pawn her ornaments.) At the reception, I explain jestingly to an affable professor from Missouri that I agreed to ignore sartorial standards for the affair because one can't really offend a Texan. Is he shocked at what should be taken, by the hypersensitive, as an ethnic slur? Fearing so, I hasten to explain that I can say so because, in some senses, I am one. I feel like former governor

Edwards of Louisiana, who some years ago was criticized for telling Cajun (that is, ethnic) jokes, but his fellow Cajuns didn't seem to mind: can't a man make fun of himself and his own?

The following day, July 14th, is one of professional duties, for which I am dressed appropriately, in *tricolore.* The day includes a superb *French Review* luncheon at the Fairmont Hotel (my choice is green enchiladas with black beans, as good as any ambrosia), followed by a stroll along the Riverwalk, visits to shops in La Villita, and an evening at the Bastille Day celebration of San Antonio. With all the Hispanic culture here—one of the most individual of Texas cities—there is still room for a bit of Gallic flavor, with "La Marseillaise" sung in a spirited fashion by a man in *bleu, blanc, rouge* and beret, and dances by the Alsatian community of Castroville, which my readers will remember as "The Little Alsace of Texas." The dancers have sewn their costumes from scratch but imported from the old country the black *coifs* or headdresses.

The next stop is Austin, where my friend Patricia Teed and I will spend a pleasant weekend together. To get there, I take Interstate 35, crowded nearly all the way. I stop only for a candy bar, bought at a gas station. I should prefer more but am discouraged by a misstep: the little town of Gruene, where I left the interstate hoping to find a café, is overflowing with weekend sportsmen, antique hunters, and adolescents looking for fishing tackle, bargains in collectibles, food, drinks, diversions, and there is no parking place, scarcely room to get by on the main street. I inquire whether a festival is in progress; oh no, this is just a summer weekend in a quaint little town, settled by Germans, that still has some of its frontier charm.

The seat of the powerful Texas legislature as well as the state bureaucracy, the university, and a substantial electronics industry, Austin wears cleanliness, prosperity, and confidence along with casual clothes. It is considered a paradise alike by country-music fans, yuppies with Mercedeses, and radicals in Birkenstocks and squaw dresses; with hundreds of live music acts on a Saturday night, countless bars and restaurants, sports on Lake Travis, and (probably) ample sources of controlled substances, it almost rivals New Orleans. It does not, however, have the latter's architectural charm or character. The wide downtown thoroughfares, deserted after business hours, are eerie, making me long for the narrow, crowded streets of the French Quarter and Uptown; and the new culture that has varnished over the city's older ways is just generic chic. Nonetheless, I am not displeased by some superb *nouvelle cuisine* Mexican food at Manuel's, nor by the jazz at the Cedar Street Café ("Sanctuary for the Soulful"), nor by a new H.E.B. supermarket, arranged in the old public-market fashion, a gastronomic Eden for the beard-and-Birkenstock set: rare flowers, dozens of coffees, unusual seafood, unknown spices, fresh breads of all sorts, and strange vegetables that look alive.

To pursue our shared taste for Texas culture, Patricia and I attend a cutting-horse competition. (Patricia, a native, has not let her natural sophistication and the urbanity she developed living in France and New York diminish her appreciation of local ways.) This demonstration of human and equine prowess is not a spectators' affair: barely a few risers to sit on, no air conditioning, no announcers, no advertisements, and, aside from family members and us, no audience. But all is done according to ceremony and rule. The participants, whether schoolchildren, teenagers, or seasoned adults, are dressed in tasteful western shirts, boots, hats, and chaps; the beasts (quarter horses), including some fine palominos, are groomed perfectly. The procedures are simple. Working against the clock, the horse and its rider must first cut two calves from a small herd that is let into the arena, then separate the two and keep the remaining calf from joining its fellows at the fence, where the herd instinct drives it. Four other riders assist by cutting off the corners, but the competing horse does the work, following and indeed anticipating the calf's moves, constantly intervening between it and the herd, accelerating, breaking, changing direction. The rider must assist by his own anticipation and deft handling of the horse, and of course he must stay mounted. This is not a rodeo: no calf is harmed, and the horses seem aware of their own skills, trotting off with pride after their act. Parents watch their children perform, spouses each other; these families are not dysfunctional, the adolescents not in the streets.

After the weekend, Patricia must return to her office. I head for Alpine, a homeplace the more cherished for being separated in time as well as miles. In all my return journeys, this is the first on which I shall approach it from Austin. One takes U.S. Highway 290 through Fredericksburg, settled by Germans, where the main street, lined with handsome nineteenth-century stone buildings in frontier style, is also known as Hauptstrasse. One can visit the Vereinkirche, see Admiral Nimitz's birthplace, shop for European and Texas antiques, and eat traditional German dishes. But I wait to eat my second breakfast until reaching the Longhorn Café in Harper, just a village. (The term "second breakfast" makes me think of an incident that took place another year on a similar journey. I'd had breakfast in Dalhart, Texas, then a second breakfast at John's Café in Texline. Having crossed then into New Mexico and, a while later, southern Colorado, and thus being in mountain time, I stopped not far over the Colorado line to get lunch. The waitress brought the breakfast menu. "No, please get me the lunch menu if possible; I've already had breakfast twice in Texas." "What are you trying to do?" she asked, "eat your way across America?")

The highway then takes one through Johnson City and past both state and U.S. historical parks and the Johnson ranch. Stopping, however, is not on my agenda.

For one thing, I do not like power, and Johnson sought it supremely. Moreover, I do not wish to reexperience the pain of the dreadful war that his administration prosecuted, badly. As for the Great Society, he is fortunate in not being here to see what a monumental failure it has been.

Highway 290 joins then a portion of Interstate 10, which I follow until it intersects past Ozona with a ranch road running south, one I have never taken before, which will lead me to another and ultimately to Highway 90 in Sanderson. Most West Texas ranch roads are well surfaced but contain numerous dips, rather than bridges, into arroyos, where, if there is heavy rain, water can run high and swiftly enough to overturn a vehicle, and where imprudent souls meet their end from time to time. No chance of rain appears now: the skies are cloudless. As for the near-total isolation of the route (even on Highway 90 west of Sanderson there will be very few other drivers), it is a risk to be run: I am no mechanic but have water, a hat, and feet, and if the car breaks down I shall walk to the nearest ranch for help. Driving here alone can't be much more dangerous than being on the streets of New Orleans late at night.

If you want to know what this terrain is like, read in Cormac McCarthy's superb *All the Pretty Horses* the episode where his characters ride from San Angelo to the Mexican border. That was in 1949, but little has changed once you get off the interstate. I head off first toward Fort Lancaster, one of a series of forts strung through West Texas during the campaigns against the Indians; the road then takes me to the hamlet of Sheffield on the edge of the Permian Basin oil patch. What homesick or deluded adventurers whom the winds of fate had blown to this desolate area remembered England's green and pleasant land and gave these appellations to places that resemble their namesakes not at all? I should like to buy a postcard in Sheffield for my friends in the British city of that name, but there is no store of any variety here—

just a few scattered shacks, some oil-field equipment, and a school-bus stop.

Alpine, I observe regretfully, looks run-down, despite numerous new houses on the north side. The dividing of Highway 90 into two one-way streets has eroded the prominence of Holland Avenue, once the central east-west artery; chain motels and other innovations threaten the older hostelries; what were mainline shops have given way to more marginal enterprises; ugly trash containers line the highway and other streets; ghastly golden arches detract further from the neat town of ten or twenty years ago. A new jail abuilding signals increased numbers of thefts, drug deals, and even occasional murders. The college, however, is prospering; I am told that some 2,200 students now attend, and I notice—oh desert miracle—an experimental vineyard on one of its slopes, the first time, to my knowledge, that any agriculture has been undertaken there or elsewhere in Brewster County, given over otherwise to deer, pronghorn, and stock—cattle, sheep, goats. The trees in town look enormous; they, as much as anything, are my measure of time. And I am happy to see again some of the familiar corners, including the Methodist church, in which Mexican ecclesiastical architecture serves felicitously the Wesleyan practice.

Dutifully, I make my rounds of visits to the few remaining friends of my mother's. One dear soul, Anne Williams, is anxious lest I get lost in town; her habits of thought come from the narrow circumscription of her life—she was originally from down Cotulla way but has lived in Alpine sixty-five years—and a protective devotion to the children, then grand- and great-grandchildren of her sister Nell. (She is also sister to the late Agátha—accent on the middle syllable—second wife of a rancher named Ed Davidson. His first wife was called Azel. I am told that all three are buried in the same plot, the wives under smaller stones at the corners, adoringly turned to face his monument.) Another acquaintance, aged ninety-five and still driving, God help us—although she no longer "rides" (her term) her friends—is similarly a good Christian woman, but one who succeeded, along with late husband and now almost-elderly son, in living more or less on the public dole, without working a day, while owning handsome family diamonds and spending much of her time playing bridge. She discusses travel with me, deploring the changes in mores and speaking of the "riffraff" who are now allowed on airplanes.

Loyce and Ralph are again my hosts. With their son Keith, badly crippled from polio (my mother tutored him when he was unable to attend school regularly) but able to carry on a career as a hospital official in Galveston and to drive across the state for family visits, we go to eat Mexican food on the other side of the tracks. This is also where the cemetery is located; Keith proposes a visit to the graves of my parents and that of his brother Kenneth, killed while working on telephone lines. The memorial stones, of pink granite, that mark my mother's and father's resting place are tasteful, appealing to both eye and fingers, although one has sunk somewhat in the sand. Nothing about my mood is pleasurable, however; absence and futility seem to inhabit the earth, the air. I understand how the poet Max-Pol Fouchet could write that, after his father's death, he ceased believing in God. Only later do I reflect that it is the eve of my mother's birthday one century before. Even if some latter-day Moliéresque doctors hadn't helped her on her way years ago, she would be dead now in any case. What of her still lives in me recognizes at least that spending eternity in a sunken tomb amid the dry sands of West Texas, visited by few, is no worse than in a grandiose mausoleum amid well-watered lawns and admired by many. Her end befits her life, characterized by incorruptible moral strength, devotion to others, and a wise acceptance, both practical and philosophical, of life's vicissitudes, including, finally, those human failings to which even she was heir.

There is more than one route from Alpine to El Paso and New Mexico, my next destination. The traditional one follows U.S. Highway 90 through Marfa (prettier than Alpine, with the elegant Paisano Hotel and a shaded courthouse square bordered by handsome churches), the hamlet of Valentine, and Van Horn, where it ends, joining Interstate 10 (a.k.a. U.S. 80), which then passes by Sierra Blanca, Fort Hancock, and Fabens. A variation is to drive to Fort Davis to the north, either directly or via Marfa, then follow State Road 118 through the Davis Mountains to Kent, where it meets I-10. This road, practically untraveled, winds through mountain passes and high pastures, past the national historical site of old Fort Davis, a state park, and the McDonald Observatory of the University of Texas, whose *Star Date* program you may have heard on public radio. This route is not a way to make good time, but time is usually not my concern when I am in West Texas, and I have sometimes elected it. A third and lengthier route takes one to Van Horn, then along State Road 54, which runs straight north toward Guadalupe Peak (elevation 8,751 feet, the highest point in Texas) and Carlsbad, New Mexico, intersecting U.S. 62 and 180 before the state line. I remember this road from 1972; it is time to try it again.

In Van Horn (accent on the first word), there is a good café I recommend, called the Smokehouse, run by people named Van Horn (no kin to the namesake of the town, as the informative menu, in the form of a tabloid newspaper, points out). It includes an automobile museum with a dozen old cars—Packards and so on—and a collection of sports memorabilia. Helmets from all twenty-eight NFL teams are displayed on a high shelf (the two expansion teams from 1995 are not yet represented at this date, nor are subsequent additions); there are four baseball pennants, including one from the Washington Senators (this collector started some while ago, or has been engaged in trading), baseball bats, a San Antonio Spurs jersey, and six portraits of Joe Torre, with the various jerseys he wore as he moved from one team to another and uniforms were redesigned; he is not from around those parts, however, coming instead from Brooklyn. All this is very well, but it is the food that counts: good coffee and a robust BLT on homemade bread, with potato chips and a watermelon slice on the side, all for around $4.50. Locals enjoy it too: in an adjacent room the Van Horn Rotary Club has begun its weekly meeting, with the singing of "Rotary, My Rotary" and "Vive la Rotary" (you can guess the tunes) above "String of Pearls" playing on the jukebox in the background.

After lunch and a fill-up, I take the state road north. The sign says "No services for 100 miles." I traverse vast stretches of cholla cactus, greasewood, salt cedar, creosote bush, and catclaw, which constitute ranches such as the Figure 2, and see little else, even after turning toward El Paso on the east-west highway, just about where one crosses into the mountain time zone (*finally,* given the meridian, about 105° west). Around Salt Flat, barely recognizable as a hamlet but on the map, for lack of anything bigger, the terrain is so alkaline and despoiled of any greenery that it is unfit even for goat ranching; but there *is* a little gas station where I purchase a cold Pepsi-Cola. The road is nearly mine. After a long stretch of almost unspoiled wilderness, with only an occasional sign ("For Sale" with a backward *s* and no more than three billboards the entire way), I reach the outskirts of what was once known on both sides of the Rio Grande as El Paso del Norte. With their car-wrecking yards, shacks, cheap bars, and heteroclite other businesses, these are shabby and tough outskirts, entirely different from the motel-and-mall stretches along the interstate. But they are not without redeeming features: Benetton has no store along this row, and one gets the impression that at least these people have *their* shabbiness, not someone else's. The highway leads me into the city's old section; somehow, I succeed in finding the interstate, which turns north and, after some fifteen miles, will carry me into New Mexico (about which readers will find more in the last essay of this volume). I have now crossed the whole of Texas, east to west—approximately 880 miles if one takes the interstate, considerably farther by my rambling route.

On the return trip from the Four Corners area and northern New Mexico, I take something of a hypotenuse down the South Plains, via Farwell, on the Texas–New Mexico line, through Muleshoe, Lubbock, Big Spring, San Angelo. Then it is the Hill Country—Fredericksburg and Austin—followed by La Grange, Columbus, and Houston. On this trip, I will have driven 4,700 miles. I have just read in the *New Yorker* Martin Amis's statement that poets don't, or shouldn't, drive. Doubtless he has in mind mostly the British, though it also holds true for some urban poets in America, denizens of New York and San Francisco. He clearly doesn't know me.

In the South Plains, I pass through the hometowns of Waylon Jennings, Dan Blocker, and other Texas luminaries. I am not an idolater of popular-culture figures, called celebrities (nor of anyone else), but, icon for icon, those from Texas are certainly no worse that those originating in California or New York (or New Orleans, to offer a comparison from my current home). Stopping in Lubbock, which always seems to happen to me, has at least one advantage: making me anticipate with pleasure the return to New Orleans. The flatness and emptiness of the Llano Estacado, impressive and heroic when one looks out at hardscrabble fields and unlimited sky, are, in town, dismaying. A massive freeway system, paid for by free-flowing federal tax dollars directed that way by the weighty Texas delegation, carries a small fraction of the traffic one would expect. Shortly after 6 P.M., I can see from my hotel room only five or six cars on Q, the six-lane main street; the so-called Civic Center, with its statue of Buddy Holly, is deserted, as is the hotel restaurant. Without the crowds, I have a sense of agoraphobia.

Then, there are the byzantine (or rather, Baptist) liquor laws. After dinner, I want to buy several bottles of Texas wine to take home: this is now a major center of viticulture, including the prizewinning Llano Vineyards. Ah, but Lubbock is dry, I am told. But how can that be, since I had wine with dinner and a beer in the bar? Perhaps the hotel has a dispensation, or selling liquor in stores is forbidden. Anyhow, I am directed to dealers outside of town, past the freeway maze; and indeed they are there, apparently doing a tremendous business. I stop at the Double T, a supermarket-style place, with two entrances and a drive-in, where clients, including obviously underage high-school girls, are lined up. The first entrance is locked, however; it is just now nine o'clock, an hour after which, it turns out, one cannot sell hard liquor, kept on that side of the store. The high-school girls go elsewhere, probably to another county (they won't settle for less than potent spirits), and I make my way to the second entrance, opening into the wine and beer section.

Do I belong here in Texas, despite the ridiculous liquor laws and other social and intellectual confines? There is more than one way to answer this, starting with the incidental, superficial attachments. Yes, in terms of cuisine: I like a place in which, at almost every café, chili and Mexican plates are available; good barbecue, like that at Al and Son's in Big Spring, is found in all parts of the Lone Star State, though just which is the best hasn't yet been agreed upon; and one need not bother, in a real Texas eatery, to say "No mayonnaise" on a hamburger, since the formula is mustard, pickles, and onion—the best in the world. At Lasserre's in Paris (readers will remember my disappointment there), when my host observed that food didn't seem to interest me much, I felt like saying, "Bring on some good Texas beans and potato salad and barbecue or enchiladas and you will see." Yes, in terms of other customs and tastes: dress is casual and relaxed, the pace often similarly so; men, many of whom wear boots and hats and still take off the latter indoors, are men; doors are open, courtesy and hospitality genuine, pretensions few. As David Kirby wrote in the *Southern Review,* a propos of a poem called "Redbeans, Rice, and a Good Radio Station," from Earl S. Braggs's *Hat Dancer Blue,* "In a world bent on photo-copying itself and then copying the copies, it is through down-home objects such as these that we tell ourselves who we are." One is not bombarded here by references to cyberspace and virtual reality; *here* are space and re-ality.

Is it not reasonable, in any case, for a thinking person who ordinarily follows city routines to withdraw occa-sionally to the country, and take there a bath of differ-ence, or similarities, as the case may be? For me, Texas *feels* right; and feeling has to count along with thinking: popular psychology can't be *entirely* wrong. Some con-sider culture determining as well as nurturing, and to that degree it would be appropriate for states to retain or take back many of the responsibilities now accruing to the federal government, with concomitant rights: indi-viduality of place and past means individuality of needs, which are best met on the local level. This is not identi-cal to Balkanism, but rather may be a deterrent to it.

But of course most of us, in a sense, belong nowhere, if deep roots are implied. Whereas, until recent decades, large numbers of Europeans still lived very close to their remote ancestral origins—and this is still true in China— no Americans, I think (and it is for them chiefly that I write), now live where their forefathers lived a thou-sand years ago; the Pueblo Indians may be descended from the Anasazi, but the latter were displaced in the twelfth century, and other tribes, including the Navajos, migrated or were uprooted after A.D. 1000. Members of the Rio Grande pueblos are among the few who can identify an ancestral home on these shores dating from even three or five hundred years ago. Furthermore, in a way, I do not really *belong* anywhere, not in Colorado: too many years have passed since my girlhood there; not in France, despite deep intellectual interests and a strong sense of identification with the French past and culture: I am not really French, after all.

Nor am I truly at home even in New Orleans, notwithstanding friends, long years and pleasure at living there, and commitment to contributing to it, however little. Even with their veneer of culture (some do see plays, attend concerts and gallery openings, occasionally buy books), the *gratin* of New Orleans society (the sort who say, "You're not from here but we like you anyway") and the chic café set are not really my circle, nor would they understand me, although some members have indicated a vague interest in my work. I do not particularly like the arty set. The ordinary locals would know even less what to do with me; do they read poetry? (But then, does anyone?) Certain successful blacks, especially some in high political office, seem concerned mostly with establishing and extending their power. Sometimes I think it is the common working blacks with whom, in my semimarginalized condition, I identify the most: they don't put on airs, at least, and some of them are trying, really trying, to improve themselves.

Yet, although for me, what Maurice Barrès, born in Lorraine, termed "la terre et les morts" are mostly in West Texas, owing to youthful experience and the permanent bonds of death, to what degree could I espouse the life reported in the Alpine *Avalanche,* the *Big Bend Sentinel,* or the *News* of Archer City, earlier and now again the home of Larry McMurtry, which reports such items as "porkers" errant in town? The question of belonging needs distinctions, clearly. I spoke earlier of the central issue of individual versus community. One really belongs among those of like mind, past and present. This mind includes for me the need *not* to belong—to retain independence of action and thought. Like the Transcendentalists, I prefer mostly inner authority. Conciliating personal and intellectual freedom with communality and human intercourse is the challenge. James Q. Wilson has argued in *The Moral Sense* that there is a shared moral feeling, or feelings, among human beings, shaped by common aspects of social structure and experience, yet this sense is and must be individual. With my family and scattered friends—including some mentioned in this essay—there is often a pleasing tangency, even overlapping of mind; yet someone whose geographic itinerary has been circuitous, as has mine, and who has struggled with the moral and literary complexities of her own career as—vicariously—of others', will find few fellow travelers, apart from those with whom communication can take place only through the printed page, since they are dead.

This leaves places. Assuming the leisure to go there, or at least to think them into presence, one can make of them almost what one wants, since, unlike human beings, they do not respond with claims and needs of their own, beyond their *fact*. It could be argued that one belongs in whatever spot, and to whatever order, will enable one the most. Imaginary places of refuge that appeal to me include Rabelais's Abbey of Thélème. Among historic retreats, I am drawn to Voltaire's Ferney and Montaigne's tower, pure of line, solid of construction, whose library represented for him, and still does for readers who consult the essays that grew out of his commentaries, as much truth and autonomy of mind as man can hope for. Paradoxically, the narrow confines of a turret, associated often with imprisonment, can also be a place of freedom, enhanced by the perspective offered by height. Among geographic settings for unlimited reflection, the mountains and the desert are in my view the finest (as readers know), though a lonely seashore can also serve.

So, when I am not in Montaigne's tower (or, my nearest equivalent, an upstairs library carrel or my residence on the seventh storey), I need space and its implications of freedom for the mind as well as the eyes. McMurtry writes: "The sky wasn't big enough for me in Virginia. . . . I need big sky." Patricia tells me that when she lived in New York, what she missed most from Texas were the thunderheads; I understand. Such an attitude can lead, of course, to escapism, isolation, and solipsism; thus Alceste, Molière's misanthrope, retreats into isolation (the "desert"), and the Romantics took refuge (at least poetically) in high mountains and isolated groves and were often insufferable to others. I do not want to think or write my fellows out of my scope and concern. But nature is, finally, our widest community. If I want the Lone Star State to claim me, it is not just because of the enchiladas or the drawl or the ingenuous friendliness. I want the widest arena for the widest thought, with shivers of plenitude under the great wind-churned skies and raveling clouds, and the warp and woof of desert stretching to a frame of purple hills.

On the rue des Ecoles, a busy street in the Latin Quarter, I am standing in front of a cinema, waiting for tickets to go on sale for an old Max Ophuls movie, which I will see shortly along with half a dozen other viewers, all young, perhaps students weary of preparing for examinations, or aficionados of film history and art. It is June: "then, if ever, come perfect days"; and this is indeed one such, with sunlight honeying the pavement and walls, and a blue breeze making curtains dance at the open windows. I am not the only one surveying this scene in apparent idleness. Across the street on an upper balcony, a German shepherd (or, as the French prefer to call the breed, an Alsatian) seated on his haunches is following intently the comings-and-goings—the passing of pedestrians, cars, bicycles, *motos,* and sometimes a cat or fellow canine, with, as an accompaniment, the steady sound of voices and engines, and the percussion of an occasional shout.

He does not appear unhappy as an urban creature, confined to an apartment for most of his hours. European city dogs are among the most content of their species, I have concluded, gaining in the exchange of a world of fields and woods for one of stone and pavement. Treated with respect and affection, if I am to believe my observations, they also have privileges not granted in the United States—access to restaurants, shops, the subway, trains, sometimes even theaters—thus having more hours of companionship with their masters and a greater range of stimulation and pleasures. (I have just found, in a lighthearted book by Peter Gethers, this gem: "The French love animals; they treat them a lot better than they treat tourists." True, true. One could, of course, point out that tourists are *people*, often Americans . . .) In short, dogs (and cats) almost have the status of citizens. As well as being convenient for their owners, this arrangement produces what are very civilized animals, less rowdy than their American counterparts, well versed in street and *métro* manners.

From the evidence, I conclude that this particular dog is a philosopher, if such a thing is possible. That the Greek word for dog, *kyn* (> Latin *canis,* whence Fr. *chien,* Eng. *canine* and *kennel*) and its companion *kynikos* (= cynic) were associated with the philosopher Diogenes encourages me in my musing: one of the meanings of *cynic* is belief that the essence of virtue "lies in self-control and independence." I have in mind, however, something more like the reflectiveness that leads to understanding and, when joined with action, to wisdom. (Blake's "Proverb of Hell" meets with my approval: "He who desires but acts not, breeds pestilence"—except that I wish to add *thinks* to *desires. Dogs, to be sure, are excepted from the obligation to *act*.) I feel no shame in acknowledging that this beast and I are alike as we watch the human comedy—or what one can see in the streets, which is a goodly amount—in the city where one of its supreme students wrote it up in dozens of volumes. There are differences, though: the dog, presumably, does not wonder what I am thinking, while I *do* wonder about him; and, just as surely, he has very limited access to the world of time and none to that of ideas, seeing life rather as flickering, transient images on a moving screen, instead of looking behind phenomena for their essences and triangulating experience, using the past, present, and one's self. (One may suppose, however, that at least he has more abstracting ability than do characters in a novel by Alain Robbe-Grillet.) He has no notion of going in search of lost time, neither satisfaction nor melancholy in cultivated reminiscence.

I, on the other hand, as I walk again through Paris, am inhabited by the past, those cold months in autumn 1957 when I was first here and learned to know the city through its tangible dimensions as well as the images that had earlier been a main course on my literary menu. Gone, of course, was the magnificent period of modernist literary and artistic blossoming—the banquet years, as Roger Shattuck termed them, of pre-1914 Paris, and the rebellious and innovative, if disabused, twenties. France in midcentury had been scarred by the two previous decades, when social strife and war had turned aside or destroyed many of the most vigorous creative impulses. That year, 1957, was still close enough to the end of World War II to be part of the *après-guerre*, politically, culturally, and economically. In Algeria, the second midcentury French colonial conflict, following almost without pause upon the first, which had ended with the defeat of France at Dienbienphu and the Geneva Accords, was raging, creating the sense that France would never get out of war. The disputatious, inefficient, sickly Fourth Republic was in its final months; it fell toward the end of my stay, in a near-revolution complete with assault forces in the streets, demonstrations, conspiracies, and an *homme providentiel,* sent as it were by destiny to pull the chestnuts out of the fire once more for his nation—a secretive, ambitious, but paternalistic figure who went to Algeria to tell the European settlers there, "I have understood you," while envisaging the liquidation of French colonial rule.

The political axes were still those of prewar and postwar, encompassing, at one extreme, Communists and socialists, at another, monarchists and other right-wingers, all militant, and various centrist parties unable to form stable coalitions. More than occasional traces remained (as still to this day) of the vicious hatred and resentment between Pétainists and Gaullists, collaborationists (or simply folk who did nothing) and Resistance partisans, so that sometimes it appeared that the war and Occupation had not ended. The economy had barely begun to emerge from the morass of the 1940s: paper was expensive and somewhat scarce (in toilets, for instance); the telephone system was primitive; housing was insufficient; comforts and facilities had often not progressed beyond nineteenth-century standards; daily necessities were high-priced; food was mediocre. The lecture halls had little or no heat. Worst of all, labor stoppages were a principal political tactic, so that electricity, already very dear, was often cut off, and *métro* strikes were so frequent that it became almost routine for me to walk across nearly half the city, from the Sorbonne to student housing on the Boulevard Jourdan.

On the cultural scene, existentialism was the rule of the day, and at the cafés in Saint-Germain-des-Prés (where drinks were more affordable than today) and on the Boulevard Saint-Michel, one could observe the rickety, flour-faced, black-clad followers of that cheery philosophy. (Perhaps it is uncharitable of me to mock their physique: if their diet was insufficient during the war, it was not their fault.) Camus won the Nobel Prize that autumn, a year after publishing *The Fall,* his masterly indictment of modern ironic man and the political and moral world that made irony an understandable, if not appropriate, response. What would be called the Theater of the Absurd was flourishing, with Ionesco's *Lesson* and *Bald Soprano* playing (as they are still today) in the tiny Théâtre de la Huchette, where they had ushered in the absurdist decade, and Beckett's humorous, though heart-wrenching, metaphysical farces on the boards. Springing from a similar epistemological and ethical skepticism, the "new novel," "anti-novel," or, in Claude Mauriac's term, "alittérature" had challenged traditional notions of plot and character and, by implication, the knowability of the world.

Cold, gloomy, often half-paralyzed (I mean the city, not myself, although sometimes the adjectives nearly suited my mood and my aching legs): how could one like the place? And yet I did, deeply. The city's beauty was still intense, the intellectual opportunities were abundant, my mind and senses were ready for them. I read, wrote pastiches of poems by Baudelaire, went to the theater, talked with fellow students and a few writers whom I met, learned to know the Left Bank well. Sharp images return in their Parisian distinctiveness—a stand in the Montsouris park where, for lack of better, I bought a dry *saucisson* sandwich that was like dentist's cotton in the mouth; a café near the Fontaine Médicis and Luxembourg Gardens, on the terrace of which I sat shivering, pulling my collar around my neck; blotchy, leafless chestnut trees, looking chilled, along the Seine; the whine of the subway wheels around a bend; the train I took for my first visit to Chartres; a bottle of perfume I had won in a dance contest during the crossing on board the *Flandre* and opened upon arrival, whose scent and name, *Ma Griffe,* indeed remain for me to this day the signature of Paris, evoking the city in Proustian recall.

Of course, Paris has changed. Why not? So have we all. Change is the law of organic and cultural life. My friends Henri and Hélène Mitterand ask me each summer what strikes me as different. All who love Paris and visit it more than once risk surprises, sometimes disturbing, and when they return later, those who were young in Paris will measure their age against their image of how it was. Just being more than two thousand years old (counting from its first founding as Lutetia) and one of the great creations of the Occident does not make the City of Light immune to modifications, certain of them striking, such as skyscrapers. In "Le Cygne" ("The Swan"), Baudelaire wrote of the melancholy of exile and alienation in a city radically altered by Baron Haussmann's urban design:

> *The Paris of the past is gone (a city's form*
> *Can change, alas, more quickly than a human heart);*
>
> *. . . . .*
>
> *Though Paris changes, in my melancholy mind*
> *Things have not moved! New platforms, palaces, and*
>   *blocks,*
> *Old neighborhoods, for me are allegories, all,*
> *And cherished memories are heavier than rocks.*

In the early twentieth century, Apollinaire, in the persona of his *mal aimé,* walked around in the vast city, whose new modernist beauty fascinated him but accentuated his unhappiness:

> *I wander through my lovely Paris*
> *Not having the heart to die there*
>
> *. . . . .*
>
> *Paris evenings drunk on gin*
> *Flaming with electricity*
> *The tramways green lights on their spine*
> *Are musicking along the staves*
> *Of rails their madness of machines*

Should one applaud this modernist transformation and its more recent sequels, or simply blame and lament, like Baudelaire, visualizing the narrow streets on the Ile de la Cité and the Left Bank as though the whole of Paris still resembled them, imagining the past, with all its flaws, as more genuine as well as more aesthetic? On balance, Paris has improved in the last forty-five years, not just for me but for millions, who are better housed, fed, clothed, warmer, have superior medical care and, generally, increased income and leisure with which to enjoy their city. And these millions count; a utilitarian in the manner of John Stuart Mill, I want the greatest good for the greatest number. (This does, of course, beg the ancient question: what is the good? Architecturally speaking, for instance, the dreadful Centre Pompidou, is, unlike the I. M. Pei pyramid in the Louvre courtyard, inherently ugly and a sore on the city's skin, no matter what enthusiasts claim.) Alcoholism, we are told, has been reduced considerably; smoking is no longer allowed in the subway and many other public places. *Métro* cars are less noisy, cleaner, more comfortable; numerous stations have been pleasantly redone; the lines extend farther. Shop windows are more attractive, the sidewalks have less filth, and much of Paris has been freshened, starting with the stone-cleaning projects under Malraux's tenure as minister of culture and continuing now, with the laser-beam cleaning of Notre-Dame. The post offices are better organized and cheerier. Even some of the functionaries have grown polite, recognizing perhaps the value of a smile, and being content enough with their lot to give it; this transformation is not, however, so generalized that it has become impossible to have a good row with an immigration official at the Orly airport. American friends tell me that one can even work without too much frustration at the new Bibliothèque Nationale de France; I'll leave this to them, since, personally, I no longer pore over dusty tomes when abroad.

To be sure, many social and economic problems remain, in Paris as elsewhere in France, among them high unemployment, mendicancy, and ethnic strife in sections with large North African populations. There are still street sweepers, but at least they now wear bright green uniforms and have green brooms—not an insignificant departure from the dreadful dust-gray of yore— and their wages are better; on the broad sidewalks of the Champs-Elysées a young woman in green drives an ingenious motorized cleaning machine with a tube like an elephant's trunk, which can be directed to pick up deftly a torn *métro* ticket or cigarette butt. It is pleasing to see that an eminent economist, writing in the *Figaro,* speaks of *ethical* standards for salaries.

Yet, like so many other human phenomena, the modernization of Paris has produced some ugly, miasmic counterreactions, as solutions such as expanding suburbs, housing projects, expressways, and thousands of automobiles create new problems. Ancient charm has been threatened or destroyed even more than in Baudelaire's day, and prosperity has brought too many people, too many consumer products. Already in the seventeenth century, the poet and satirist Nicolas Boileau complained about the congestion of Paris streets; today he would discover a different magnitude of traffic problems. The art of the city's great museums—the city itself *as* museum—attracts so many busloads of tourists that, although I walk by the Louvre every day on this visit, I have not brought myself to enter the new wing, veritably besieged. Here as elsewhere, the reign of technology is often felt as dehumanizing, and low common denominators of products and styles, vulgar advertising, and linguistic barbarisms such as "Le Drugstore" have not established a true sense of broad communality, but rather have created merely a superficial, ephemeral universalism, and tend to alienate people from their language and traditions, whose decline impoverishes them even if they do not know it.

Paris has resisted moderately well, however, the leveling of distinctive culture that characterizes much of the developed world, assimilating the new with style and preserving much of the graceful old. Since the skyscrapers are at or near the periphery, they have not destroyed the quaintness of the art district around the Ecole des Beaux-Arts, the character of the Latin Quarter, or the proportions and lines of the city's most beautiful and best-known prospects—the Champs-Elysées, the Ile de la Cité with Notre-Dame, the Ile Saint-Louis, Montmartre, the Place du Panthéon, the Champ-de-Mars and Eiffel Tower. The occasional Burger King and McDonald's ("Macdo") eateries are partly disguised by being embedded architecturally in already-existing structures—no giant golden arches and drive-in windows. The linden and chestnut trees still grace the boulevards, newspaper kiosks and bookstalls along the Seine do a steady business, the excursion boats glide along the river as in the past; one feels that the rhythm of *An American in Paris* is still right, the flavor of Hemingway's movable feast still there.

The movie over, I walk down the Boulevard Saint-Michel, turn left at the Boulevard Saint-Germain, then take the rue de l'Ancienne-Comédie (thus going by the Procope Café, the oldest in Paris, where Voltaire and other philosophes passed the time) toward the Seine, pass the Institut, walk along the *quais,* cross the Pont du Carrousel, and, having traversed the Louvre courtyard, stop for a late-afternoon drink on the sidewalk of the Musset, a café near the Place du Palais-Royal and the Comédie-Française. Like almost any of thousands of cafés and *brasseries* (fewer, though, than in the past—an unhappy effect of changed habits and economy), this spot is favorable for people-watching. Here, as on the Champs-Elysées, I will get a large sampling of tourists and businesspeople, whereas at lunchtime at the Brasserie Balzar in the Latin Quarter, it was the Sorbonne crowd, and yesterday, near the quiet Bourdelle Museum beyond Montparnasse, one saw strictly neighborhood folk. Since I have no one to converse with, except in imagination, looking and listening—eavesdropping, if you will—are in order. (I do not mind being alone, though I miss my daughter, often my companion in Paris but occupied in New York this summer.) Like that dog, I am an inveterate student of passers-by. After all, I am a writer. Whereas Balzac believed that a person's lodging told all about him, one can take the converse position and try to derive the profession, the lodging, the habits from physical appearance—sex and age, of course, gait, clothing and other accouterment, companions, snatches of speech. As readers know, I often look at shoes; they reveal a great deal. My skills have been developed by long years in New Orleans, not a mediocre spot for studying one's fellows; but Paris—far larger, more varied, with greater street life—is still more favorable.

Baudelaire, the poet of *tableaux parisiens,* spoke of taking a "bath of crowds." In a sense, that is what I am doing, slightly on the edge here at the café, where I can take in the human presence without being jostled in a packed bus or having to pick my way along the narrow sidewalks among couples walking abreast, children, dogs, open umbrellas, baby carriages, old women, and other impediments to progress. I like a little distance between myself and others (thus, the reluctance to go to the Louvre with several thousand tourists)—although I can put up with a subway crowd as well as anyone else, and social snobbery strikes me as being base. Some actors in this urban tableau pass by; some sit and converse or watch the others, and sip their *apéritifs.* By and by, the roles will be reversed as the current clients leave to go about their business (figurative, for the most part, at this hour—but *some* have to work) and others arrive; few Parisians are so deprived that they cannot afford a drink on a café terrace.

The question arises whether my observations are meaningful in any way. They could be considered, after all, as a random collection of sights and sounds, without any underlying rationale or coherence, except by their co-presence at this moment and in my perceptions; what difference does it make that I note, among a swarm of sensory data, a businessman carrying a plastic sack, two chattering schoolgirls in plaid, some Japanese wearing suits and eyeglasses, a chic woman in a short skirt seated near me, with a sharp nose and chin, a car parked on the sidewalk, some hideous white plastic footgear, an Indochinese kitchen helper coming out from behind the bar, an odor of diesel fuel? The dog could notice almost as much. But I said he was a philosopher; observation is not unrewarding. This is, after all, the *real,* and our interaction with the real shapes what we know and become. From the ordinary sights of Paris streets and boulevards—steeples, street corners, cafés, umbrellas, lampposts—Impressionist painters and their followers created a way of seeing and added to our visual dictionary. Almost any real will do; Raymond Aron told Sartre that from an apricot cocktail one could draw an entire philosophy. What is before me happens to be particularly fine, an appealing slice of life in a city laden with history, where beauty is often paramount (despite the awful footgear), a place architecturally splendid and culturally rich (I will see a dozen plays and films before leaving; visit bookstores, churches, parks and gardens, and more than a half-dozen museums; attend concerts; indulge in food as art; drink good wine; meet friends, of course; and walk along the Seine day after day to enjoy the perspectives).

There is another dimension here, something extraordinary but which I cannot quite call the exotic. After all, I have visited Paris many times; there are no wild beasts, except in the Jardin des Plantes and, in museums, in the form of those painters called the Fauves, no strange flora except in horticultural displays, no pampas, steppes, desert, and if you discount the bizarre getup of some students and artists in the Latin Quarter and Montparnasse, as well as some peculiar fashion trends in *haute couture,* little unusual garb is displayed except by a few visitors from Africa. Let us call what I have in mind the *marvelous*—represented in the ancient world by the Seven Wonders, and akin to that power which in classical plays and poetry makes the gods appear and amazing feats take place. Not that I expect divine apparitions here, although, with its many neoclassical structures and sculptures, the site would be fitting, and such legends as the decapitated Saint Denis carrying his head, such statuary as the gilded equestrian Joan of Arc at the Place des Pyramides and the gargoyles on Notre-Dame remind us constantly of the supernatural and wondrous. It is rather that the whole city is a marvel—its deep roots, which antedate Julius Caesar, its tangible layers of time, its blend of styles and peoples (Celt, Latin, Germanic, now others), its cultural wealth, and, perhaps most of all, the fact that it was not destroyed by those wars which, through aerial bombardment or street fighting, razed much of Berlin, Cologne, Frankfurt, Dresden, Rotterdam, Coventry, Rheims, and other European cities. The envious Kaiser Wilhelm and his armies never *did* get to Paris, thanks to the Battle of the Marne, which Barrès compared to Joan of Arc's victories; Hitler's troops got there all too easily and ruined one way or another tens of thousands of Parisian lives, but happily, thanks to strongly Francophile Germans in positions of power, left almost intact, even upon withdrawing, the gorgeous city and its bridges. That it is here to be enjoyed, that we are here to enjoy it, is a double wonder.

As for relationships with my fellow human beings, they can, despite what contemporary naysayers would assert, be established by this dallying at a café and other marginal participation in the life of a city to which I belong only by elective affinity. (One of those naysayers I have in mind is Sartre, who makes fun in *Nausea* of the Self-Taught Man's sentimental but solitary humanism. Despite his rejection of conventional social solidarity and the milk of human kindness, however, Sartre enjoyed life tremendously, whereas generally, as the example of Louis-Ferdinand Céline shows, cynicism and hostility do not serve their disciples well.) True, one cannot simply think into existence a communality of spirit, much less the means to achieve common goals: the multiplicity of city phenomena does not create a whole through my thinking it, but only by the will of most of its agents. But clearly, this will is present, and has been for centuries:

one does not have to reinvent the idea of the *polis,* which in its Parisian form (suburbs included) is composed of some ten million people, one-quarter of the French labor force, and countless visitors. As the home of the principal Enlightenment philosophes and the center of the Revolution and its sequels, Paris cradled the idea of popular republican government; the blue and red added to the white of the Bourbons to create the French tricolor flag were the city colors. The city is thus emblematic of as well as constituted by popular union. To observe life here is, in short, to be present at—perhaps moved by—a remarkable social organization as well as an extraordinary achievement in urban design. While I cannot, by labor or any contribution, including the not-inconsiderable money with which I part here, graft myself onto the seemingly organic life of Paris (although shared language, which is almost as thick as blood, nearly makes it possible), it is not inconsequential, for myself and others, that I embrace it sympathetically. Admiration, recognition, open movements of the mind are more than homages.

Altogether, this has been a day of varied pleasures and those *petites joies* that the singer Georges Brassens identified as constituting happiness. The cocktail hour can easily be prolonged: it will not be dark until past ten, when, finally, dimming light above the rooftops will turn purplish, then fade out. Since morning, I have gathered—for the museum of remembrance—a goodly sampling of beautiful city vistas and the various arts and pleasures cultivated here. I have seen, tasted, heard, and smelled Paris and felt it in my feet (fortunately, I am wearing low-heeled shoes with rubber soles, though not Nikes) through its graveled walks and uneven paving stones, like those that jolted Proust into remembering St. Mark's Square in Venice and making his elaborate journey into himself and time. Now, the city is sailing full-skied into evening, continuing its long voyage through history, which we share but briefly. A splendor, surely, whose experience, like all experience, is portable in reflection—but to whose reality its admirers, even when rich with memories, need to return, to hear with freshly tuned ears the new variations on its classic themes, and see its perspectives again according to its changing light and one's own. Over my mind, at the juncture of two multilayered geologies, a city's and an individual's, a smooth, even feeling falls. I can imagine that Paris will recognize me, next time.

Perhaps all of life is an interlude—a bird's brief flight across a smoldering sky or, as Nabokov wrote, the space between two voids. Within that interlude are others, great and small, bounded by, or constituted by, circumstances and events both ordinary, such as the arrival of summer vacation, and extraordinary, such as taking up a new career, and creating those watersheds mentioned at the outset of this volume. Occasionally, hindsight alone identifies an interlude as such, but often one is aware that the present is somehow distinctive, separated from what precedes and what follows by clear boundaries imposed by others, chosen by oneself, or resulting from the course of nature and human time. Time, indeed, defines us all as it enables us. My British interlude in 1996—and, within it, shorter interludes or pauses— offered a different way of being with others in *their* world—human and natural—of sensing *my* world, of feeling time pass.

The official term for the clocks I followed is Greenwich mean time, the mean solar time at the Greenwich prime meridian, constituting the standard for calculating time elsewhere in nearly the entire world—the name commemorating the former observatory through which the zero longitude line passes in that London outer borough. But I think of it as British Time—the hour that the British Isles share with few other places in Europe, since most westerly nations of the Continent (Spain, France, the Lowlands) have chosen, for reasons of economics and general convenience, to set their clocks the same as more easterly nations such as Germany and Poland. British Time is also *my* time, that is, the months I spent there, living more or less as an Englishwoman, and the daily schedule (be careful to pronounce that *shedule*), its contents contingent on the hour, of course, and often on the meteorological conditions. It is a pity that the English word *time*—in its general sense—does not, unlike its French counterpart, signify also *weather,* for such a double meaning would serve me well. Always interested—perhaps as another legacy from my youth in the American West—in the temperature, winds, precipitation, and anticipated changes (we used to watch blue northers blow across the Davis Mountains from the Permian Basin), and a faithful follower of the television meteorologists in New Orleans, especially Carl Arredondo, who can be counted on to give not only our weather but also that in his native state of Texas, whence ours usually comes, I was no less preoccupied with weather in England.

Quite rightly so. I arrived from New Orleans in South Yorkshire in January, to spend the semester as a visiting research professor at the University of Sheffield, and stayed through one of the most severe winters in decades, marked by heavy snows and extreme stubbornness; the tardy spring could not settle in until about the twenty-fifth of May. (The month of January was among the coldest on record. March had 62 percent less sunshine than the average—and how much sunshine do you think there usually is in March in Yorkshire?) I took up residence in a district of Sheffield named Broomhill. Sheffield, sometimes called the Rome of the North, is a very hilly city, with seven principal eminences as well as five rivers, which nourished the Industrial Revolution. Having no car, thus using busses or my feet to get around, living on a steep road called Sale Hill (the *hill* part being apt), and without Wellingtons to keep out slush or shoes with cleats that help one stay upright on ice, I was often concerned in the morning about the challenges of getting down the flight of concrete steps in front of my flat, staying on my feet, perhaps even *dry* feet, and making it down the incline to the bus stop, thence to the Arts Tower, where the Department of French was located. The challenge was repeated for the return at the day's end, a very dark end in January and February. I could walk home—*uphill* all the way—or I could wait in the freezing wind for a bus that ground up slowly through the traffic at that hour from the City Centre, but past the bus stop where I got off footwork still awaited me. This was especially true on days when I had to get off before my usual stop to pop in at the pharmacy or the small Somerfield supermarket; after getting my supplies, I would lug them in plastic sacks up Sale Hill. I would say, "lug them like New Orleans bag women," except that *they* usually have carts and are *always* on level ground.

Once in my flat, until the milder days finally did arrive, I first would attempt to get the heating working enough to move the temperature up from around 54 degrees to 58 degrees, maybe even 60 degrees. This heating, called "central" and thus evoking images of comfort, was supposed to be regulated by a thermostat and distributed through radiators in each of the cramped (and quite unaesthetic) rooms. The radiators did indeed receive such warmth as could be enticed from the gas unit by the thermostat, but basically the system did not work well and the product was quite inadequate for the ill-insulated "purpose-built" flat, with large picture windows and, because of its location, particularly exposed to the cruel winds, like King Lear on the heath. I would also turn on the oven in hopes that the temperature in the kitchen would rise at least a degree or so.

I then took off gloves, overcoat (purchased years ago in Chicago and about as heavy as you can get), beret (which had been pinned down against the wind), muffler, and blazer, and put on an old L. L. Bean cardigan and a silk scarf around my throat. I usually wore trousers of some sort, but if I had put on a skirt it was replaced by heavy denims. Then it was time to start the tea kettle. Yes, tea; I drank rivers of it, alternately sipping and warming my hands around the cup or pot. If shoes were wet, they would be put to dry in the kitchen. Much of the time, however, I wore sturdy oxfords bought at Marks and Spencer, truly amazing footgear that compensated for their total lack of charm by being impermeable to water (good even in a light snow) and—I now see, at some years' remove—apparently indestructible by anything less than a truck. But sometimes, because there was a guest in the department or a little social event, or I was to perform in some way, or just through vanity, I wore less sensible shoes, regretting it later, perhaps.

After tea, it was time to see to supper, which some of my English friends might have called my high tea, except that it was only marginally British, sometimes not at all. I unloaded the Somerfield plastic sacks and started a few preparations. Often I bought canned shrimp from Taiwan, chicken or smoked sausage, rice, and some spices and attempted an imitation of jambalaya. Or I found Old El Paso products—a popular, though not outstanding, line of Tex-Mex foods, in this case produced in Holland—and, sometimes using British beef, supposedly tainted, I prepared tacos or enchiladas. (International trade is truly a wonderful thing.) In April, when Patricia flew over from Austin to London to meet me, she brought me various Texas goodies and boxes of Zatarain's prepared New Orleans meals: jambalaya, gumbo, and red beans and rice. I made those last for more days than the producers expected, stretching the mixes with extra rice and shrimp. While things were cooking, I uncorked a bottle of the wine I had hauled from Somerfield and went into the sitting room to watch the news on the BBC.

That is, after some weeks. In the first month or so of my stay, I could not get the large, hotel-type television set to work. It was, in fact, one of *six* appliances or gadgets that malfunctioned or simply wouldn't turn on, at least at first: washer—filled with the previous tenant's filthy water; radio; electric bar heater; shower; can opener; and the TV. Trouble with the can opener produced a cut thumb and near starvation in the first days; I distrusted the electric heater; and the shower never did work, so that I had to sit in the tub, which kept its cold the entire season. Five weeks after my arrival, I had become well enough acquainted with an amiable colleague to broach the subject of malfunctions, and she and her husband (the same friends who traveled with me another year in the West) offered his services, those of an engineer. After much probing around, at first no more successful than my attempts, he discovered the secret switch to turn on the beastly machine. So thenceforth I could watch the six o'clock news, or if I wanted to have some companion sound before then, could turn on the radio, which I'd finally managed to master.

The BBC news is the best I have seen in any nation. Good BBC English, of course; and, thanks to the television tax, one gets a half-hour with no commercials, no interruption other than announcement of the time of day. Just as important, the presenters simply *read* the reports, avoiding—unlike newscasters in the United States—comments, grimaces, grins, laughter, redundant summaries, and other interjections and significant looks that we could well do without. A condensed weather report closes the broadcast, about 6:28. Then I could have a half-hour of *Look North,* the "local" news for the area of Lincolnshire and Yorkshire, including the regional weather. I could also get, on radio, a very detailed weather report including tide tables and wind-and-wave facts from a network of buoys around Great Britain. No sailor myself, I nevertheless delighted in the meteorological and nautical precision, leading to thoughts of men out then in the same sort of weather, often threatening, that has characterized the Channel, North Sea, Irish Sea, and Atlantic for as long as anyone knows— and to hopes for everyone's safe arrival in a haven.

It was time then to check the pot on the stove or oven dish, refill the wine glass, and pick up the newspaper. I confess to having drunk in Sheffield enormous quantities of the fruit of the vine. One is told that alcohol doesn't *really* warm the body, merely creating the illusion of comfort, but if one *believes* one feels less miserable, isn't that something? The newspaper I had purchased at the start of the day, across from the bus stop, in a store that served as newsstand, stationer's, and post office for Broomhill. I bought the *Independent,* the *Daily Telegraph,* sometimes the *Times,* or all three, and read them almost word for word, royal agendas and obituaries included. This took much of the evening, of course, some before supper, some during, some afterward.

Now, this is quite contrary to my habits at home in New Orleans, where the evening is devoted, if not to friends, to some sort of work or serious reading. But at home I have good lighting—suitable for consultation of papers laid out on a table—and a computer, and my research materials, reference books, personal papers, and so on, whereas at the Broomhill flat I had not even a dictionary, so that research was out of the question. It was hard even to write by hand; the small dining table was the only suitable surface, and I had to push aside the place mat to lay out paper. So instead I pored over newspapers and magazines, occasionally read a war novel for my main project, sketched out poems in rough draft, wrote lap postcards and scrawled letters to friends and family, listened to music on BBC radio, and stared out the window. Eventually, such staring proved rewarding. For one thing, after some days there, I discovered not very far away an imposing high-rise Forte Crest hotel, the existence of which I had been unaware of at first because it had been utterly disguised by fog. (My block of flats was called Tower View; it was no tower itself, so I wondered whether we were supposed to view the hotel, or the high-rises of the university in the other direction. Did they really count as a "view"?) Similarly, I found—when the clouds and fog deigned to lift a bit— that Sheffield at night was lovely, its golden lights spreading from hilltops down the slopes into the river valleys—brilliant fruit in an undulating grove. Then, ultimately, as the season wore on, there appeared some evening sunlight and suggestions of blue sky.

It will be thought that BBC or commercial television could have provided entertainment for the evening, as an alternative to the newspaper. This proved not to be so. Are all the good British series sent abroad for foreign consumption? Combing the listings day after day, I found little of quality or appeal; such shows as *East-Enders* and *Neighbours* are not my style, nor the other series playing that season; discussions and displays of antiques have very little attraction for me, and despite my concern and fondness for animals, I cannot watch every evening a show about training hunting dogs. So, the newspaper read, the wine gone, and the washing-up done, and the silence of a nineteenth-century Sheffield suburb (muffled often by snow) surrounding me—someone accustomed to hearing the sounds of St. Charles Avenue day and night—I usually retreated into silence and solitude, often morose, quite Baudelairian ("Quand le ciel bas et lourd pèse comme un couvercle" ["When the low and heavy sky weighs down like a lid"], as the poet wrote in "Spleen"). Sometimes I descended so far as to read British mystery novels in bed, swaddled in nightclothes (undershirt, Land's End flannel pajamas, old sweater, flannel dressing gown, wool socks) and in a nest of covers. Torticollis the following day was the rule.

The bed covers warrant some remarks. Certain close friends already know that I have a phobia concerning goose-down comforters, quilts, eiderdowns, *édredons, couettes,* and duvets. I hate the blasted things. (Would someone like to name this phobia and write it up in a mental-health journal? A case to be cited, in addition to mine, would be that of Queen Elizabeth II, who, according to the *Daily Telegraph,* demands blankets rather than duvets in hotel rooms booked for her.) The disadvantages of comforters usually include such thickness that they can't be tucked in or folded; their slippery quality, so that they slide off in the night and leave one half exposed; their reluctance to nestle close and fit around the sleeper's neck, unlike blankets; and their weight, which is unpleasant at best and often numbs my toes. Weight without warmth—that's their motto. The British are wedded to duvets; Marks and Spencer and Cole Brothers' department stores had a large stock of them, and one can rely on finding them in many hotels and in the guest rooms of otherwise gracious hosts. In Germany, scarcely any other covering exists, as travelers will attest: summer or winter, the beds are furnished with only a bottom sheet and a duvet wrapped in a cotton sack sewn fast, so that in the warmer seasons the sleeper must choose between being nearly smothered under the thing or having no cover at all, and in winter must rely on it solely. And these are supposedly rational peoples, one of whom, the English—like their Welsh and Scottish neighbors—has sheep, it would seem, in nearly every field (at least until lately, when the disastrous epidemic of hoof-and-mouth disease decimated the flocks).

When I took possession of the furnished flat on Sale Hill, what I found as bedding were a pair of sheets, two flimsy blue comforters or duvets, stuffed with cotton only, and, happily, one yellow blanket. I put the latter next to the sheet and me, but, temperatures being what they were, still had to superimpose the blue comforters. The next morning, I was numb from cold and senseless weight. A day or so later, in a terrific windstorm that preceded our first big snow, I walked (not yet having learned the bus routes) to the City Centre and bought two wool blankets in the "Ancient Campbell" plaid at Cole Brothers'. (It was the same day on which I went to register with the South Yorkshire Police as an alien.) They are travel blankets, not large enough for an ordinary bed, meant perhaps for a picnic in inclement weather, or an invalid's outing, or shipboard use, or a cold journey. My bed wasn't ordinary, however, being a narrow and foreshortened berth; they fit well. One blanket did indeed travel with me; as a precaution, I usually stuffed it into a backpack or suitcase when I went elsewhere. The duvets were then stored away in a cupboard over the clothes closet. Cold in bed I remained, but at least my feet did not turn numb and I had the reassuring feel of wool close around my neck. On extremely cold nights, I used improvised bed warmers—cooking pots heated in the oven and placed among the bedclothes for some minutes before I retired.

In the mornings, starting around eight, I would rise, turn on water for coffee, attempt to get some heat out of the furnace and the stove, and dress in a trice, often using underwear that had been prewarmed on the feeble heat of a radiator. Eight was late for me: at Tulane, I would have been seated in my office by that hour, beeing around among papers or making plans for the day; but in the Arts Tower, arrival at nine or well after seemed to be the rule. Might this be an effect of the geography and climate? In the heart of winter, it was still dark when day should have begun, and on many days snow was swirling in great tornadoes and ice covered the ground. *Everyone* seemed reluctant to venture forth from home. True, I am *frileuse,* and Sheffielders certainly took the cold better than I; not having to endure five-month subtropical summers, as we do in New

Orleans, their bodies have learned at leisure to keep their heat. Those I knew, moreover, had cars and warmer houses. But many complained of the harsh winter and late spring, and surely it was not only as a courtesy to me.

So, fortified by milky coffee, juice, and toast with marmalade, and muffled against the cold, I forced myself to step out, walked down the hill, got the newspaper and posted my letters, waited for the bus or, on better days, walked the mile to the university, took the lift (since I dreaded the paternoster—a sort of dumbwaiter for human beings) to the seventh floor of the Arts Tower, and resumed research and writing. Though its windows were large and exposed to the north winds—indeed, to all breezes, the forecourt it faced being whirl-wind-prone—my office was much warmer than the flat. And it is a pleasure to note that such comfort was produced in part by the burning of trash, the city of Sheffield having found it efficient to recycle rubbish for power. (Yet one is told in America that running a city on recycled materials is a fantasy. When will this position be abandoned?) This daily routine lasted for approximately five months, with interruptions for visits to Scotland and Wales, long weekends in London, and, in late May, a trip to Paris; it was resumed briefly twice in the summer, after a four-capital tour in central Europe and, later, three weeks in Normandy.

But why in heaven's name had I left my familiar university routine, my friends, and a pleasant and comfortable abode in the Garden District of New Orleans, where most winter days are mild and many are sunny, and gone to Sheffield? Because I was invited. But cannot one decline an offer, with polite expressions of regret? When, however, fate offers what appears to be a gift, one should accept it, unless prudence, honor, or charity dictates otherwise. Who would say no, furthermore, to a position in which one is received with courtesy, furnished with an office, computer, and library card, and paid to read, write, give an occasional lecture or presentation, and sign "Sheffield" after one's articles?

I had visited England numerous times before, starting in the late 1950s, and had seen the steel city previously, having been asked to give a guest lecture there one May, in what turned out to be a period of blue skies. Department members had extended a most cordial welcome, and despite its being in the Midlands, I had been charmed by the place, a sort of English Pittsburgh of a half-million or so (plus suburbs and populous towns nearby), its rivers cleaned up, its industry modernized. Its western edge, moreover, is bordered by a vast green belt, strictly protected, adjacent to the Yorkshire moors and the Peak District National Park, one of the prize conservation areas of England. Even the appellation "Red Sheffield" did not bother me, and the music (Halle Symphony Orchestra from nearby Manchester, Lindsay Quartet), theaters, and museums, especially the Ruskin Gallery, were an attraction. If Ruskin had liked it, or thought it worth investing in on behalf of the working man, could I not do so? And it is two hours and a few minutes from London, by trains that run every hour. I was born in the West: two hours are nothing.

Moreover, there was the appeal of adventure. Adventure is relative to the subject: for some, it involves climbing the highest peak on each of the seven continents; for others, it may be pursued in the streets of New Orleans late at night; for a few, it means a little excursion, or just staying at home, the demands and rewards of the quotidian being as much as their bodies or psyches require or can endure. Moderation in all things, I say; Everest does not attract me, but I was drawn by a modest adventure involving change of scene and climate, different ways of organizing the routine, new friends, proximity to a great city and many splendid sites of nature and architecture, and the challenge of doing a great deal while being obliged to do nothing.

Then, perhaps, I was doing it for my father. He would

have been greatly pleased on my account, and would have understood my willingness to swaddle myself in layers of heavy clothing and carry sacks of groceries up the hill in the biting wind as the price for being in England—he who loved it and had never felt more at home than there, though he also had endured a harsh English winter in the early 1960s. My parents and I had spent some delightful days together on that island in the summer of 1961 and 1962 and again in 1967, doing London, going down to Kent, stopping at pubs and inns, seeing Canterbury. Surely, remembering how much he had wished to return in his retirement, I could not have refused the opportunity. Everything good that I did and saw there, from writing poems and scholarly stuff through meeting friends for a meal, enjoying galleries and the theater, and touring villages, the great cathedrals, and the Scottish lochs and moors, belonged to him in some sense. What else can one do for the dead but live, and live well, if possible?

The Yorkshiremen as well as the university staff were lovely to me ("Yes, luv," says the bus driver in a friendly way when I ask him whether he is going all the way to Manchester Road, by Sale Hill). Dour—that's their winter climate, some of their landscape, but not their character. Colleagues and secretaries offered practical assistance, invited me to dinner at their homes or for a pub meal, organized receptions, took me into Derbyshire and on more distant excursions, listened to my accounts of small vexations, shared information and literary talk, and were uniformly gracious. People whom at the time I had never met phoned from London to welcome me; a retired Sheffield couple whose name I had not even heard invited me to dinner on the recommendation of one of these other unknowns.

I appreciated also the presence and friendliness of Sheffielders who remained anonymous. A creature of habit, and passing, as you have seen, by the same route nearly every day, my cheeks raspberry-red and my nose dripping, I became a well-known fixture of Broomhill. "A nation of shopkeepers"—well, the shops of Fulwood, Whitham, and Glossop Roads were my lifeline, furnishing not only the means to procure life's necessities but also the daily human contacts without which I would wither. The newsstand/stationer's/post office; Somerfield Supermarket; Boot's, the chemist's; Blackwell's bookstore; Williamson Hardware; the Oxfam Store (to which I gave castoffs at the semester's end); a gift shop and some dress shops; the Victoria wine outlet; two butchers; a bakery; three greengrocers; numerous banks; two travel agencies; hairdressers and barbers; two other newsstands; a fishmonger's; various eateries and three pubs; a betting parlor; the cleaner's; and miscellaneous shops—all these were crowded into what we would designate as a few blocks, a bit like parts of Magazine Street in New Orleans or the little business section of a Texas town such as Alpine (except that it had neither tavern nor betting parlor).

The closest greengrocer knew me well by sight—and by accent. I don't think we ever understood each other much; I would simply pick my flowers, vegetables, and fruit, and hand him a five-pound note—more than enough—so that he could give me change and I would not have to ask him to repeat the price once again, and he would not need to deal with my pronunciation either. Newspapers and stamps were easy to buy: I knew what they cost. With a repairman who came to fill in the ceiling in my flat, where the plaster and beaverboard were caving in, there was more difficulty. He could see the problem, of course, and worked on it without my assistance, linguistic or other, but, having nearly finished, he asked me if I had an "over." I did not quite understand—something to put *over* the filled-in spot? Finally I understood that he was speaking of a vacuum cleaner—a Hoover, that is—with which to sweep up bits of plaster.

At Woodcock Travel Agency, *every* employee and the

manager knew me by name, and I knew them as JoAnn, Claire, Jane, and so on, for I was one of their best clients that year, purchasing travel packages for Scotland, Wales—for two people—and the tour in central Europe, and buying railroad tickets as one might lottery tickets, week after week, and three cross-Channel passages. Their patience with me was exemplary. I was not the sole familiar of the place, of course; to Sheffielders, the appeal of Spain, Greece, the Canary Islands, and Florida was particularly strong throughout the winter. When I first went in, to get a "weekend break" package for London, JoAnn asked me where I was from. "New Orleans," I replied, stressing, as one should, the *Or* and doubtless drawling a bit. "Where?" For effect, I tried it again, with the same result. Finally I smiled and explained I meant New Or*leens*. They wanted to know, of course, as bitter gusts blew in each time the door was opened, what could have led me to forsake that balmy and exotic clime in favor of Yorkshire in winter.

My visits to London were welcome intervals, at once time out and time in—that is, *in* the quintessential experience available only in the capital, about which Samuel Johnson said that to tire of London was to tire of life itself. I went once a month—twice for conferences, once to give a lecture, once to meet Patricia (and we had ten days that time, it being Easter), and once just because it was high time again. With Patricia, the order of the day was touring; she had not been to England before, so it seemed imperative to do some introductory sightseeing. We also took in plays and went to Leeds Castle in Kent, and even had a coach tour of London. On one of the weekend-break packages I had bought from Woodcock's, we went to Llandudno, in northern Wales, and stayed in the dilapidated Castle Hotel, with accommodations and a manager that must have been the model for *Fawlty Towers*.

On the other visits, I was for the most part by myself,

except for a few hours spent at the conferences and drinks or meals with friends, including a visiting couple from Catalonia, an old art critic, and a retired professor from Glasgow who continues her scholarly activities in London. On each visit, I spent some time at the British Library, looking up things unavailable in Sheffield. Plays and exhibits filled much of the time; I took in as many art shows as possible and saw a play a day, getting my half-price ticket each noon at the booth at Leicester Square. One can't have too many—that's my view. The old and the new both had appeal: *Macbeth* and *The Taming of the Shrew*, a Feydeau farce, and the powerful war play *Observe the Sons of Ulster Marching to the Somme*, for instance. Stopping in at a Wren or Butterfield church, turning up an unfamiliar street, looking for an Italian restaurant, popping into a bookshop now and then—it was easy to fill the two or three days available each time. In June I managed to get to Kew Gardens, a delightful discovery.

Furthermore, in London I was generally *comfortable*. The climate is milder than that of Sheffield; one notices the difference immediately. Much getting-about takes place in the tunnels and tubes underground, away from sleet and wind. Most important, I had a cozy hotel room, usually at the Kennilworth on Great Russell Street, right near the British Museum. For the weekend-break price, I got only a small single (always the same room), but the shower worked and the place was attractive and, in particular, well heated, with a radiator that gurgled and hissed pleasantly day and night. Moreover, the bed had a sufficient supply of wool blankets. So, you might say, I went to London to get warm. Even the chilly and dark London evenings in winter were not unpleasant for me—doubly a visitor, from Yorkshire and Louisiana. Come nightfall, after a visit to an exhibit or a matinée, or before an evening performance, the comfort was prolonged in the bar, looking onto Bloomsbury Street, where, like a river during spring thaw, pedestrians, cabs, lorries, private cars, and especially busses, red, green, and gray, streamed toward New Oxford Street, honking, splashing, stopping abruptly; and I could sit there in comfort, dry, warm, in front of a large glass of wine and a plate of sandwiches or bowl of tomato (tom*ah*to) soup, and, if I chose, eavesdrop on the other customers, mostly Brits, some Americans, some Germans, appreciating, I trust, the *gemütlichkeit* of the setting.

I had no trouble, really, as a woman alone. The British respect order and as a rule know how to behave. During my first visit, I stayed near King's Cross, at a very good hotel, but not so close to St. Pancras and King's Cross stations as I had supposed. The walk back from the tube late, after the theater, was a bit lonely and the neighborhood not the best, but my deliberate stride and fast pace stood me in good stead; or maybe it was that there was no danger at all. Once, in the Strand, while waiting for the Aldwych Theatre to open, I popped into a crowded pub—a bright and really very acceptable place—and found myself elbow-to-elbow with someone who did not read my character at all well, even when, in civil, if firm, terms, I did my western best to convey it to him. I don't flirt; you don't make passes; "No, thank you" means no—those are the rules. They apply to those of all stations; I am no respecter of persons. This understanding of manners should allow one to go almost everywhere deemed "public," except for clubs, athletic facilities, and other sites designated solely for men, women, or others who, so long as they do no clear harm, certainly have the right to band together and amongst their own kind. Whether from some general outdated view on what is appropriate for the fair sex or just boorishness, women should not be made to feel uncomfortable in theaters, restaurants, inns, even places that serve spirits; to seize upon a woman alone who enters a gas station, restaurant, or bar (so long as it is not a "specialized" one, like those in the French Quarter of New Orleans, where pickups are the purpose) and treat her as prey is as ill bred, though not so destructive, as taunting a black man who has entered the wrong neighborhood in a southern city.

Was I really on, or in, British Time? Of course, though that does not make me English; indeed, that time was, I have said, an *interlude*. When I got back to England from my trip to Paris and other stays on the Continent in the summer, I was happy to set my watch again back one hour, getting away from *double* daylight saving time to something closer to the original mean. And it was always with pleasure that, returning by train from London or, occasionally, Leeds, Doncaster, or Manchester, I recognized the outlying villages of Sheffield and then, as we drew closer, glimpsed the Arts Tower and the high-rise housing estates, ill designed as they were, near the station; I was home and could go catch the Bus 60 that would take me almost to Sale Hill. As Sartre and other philosophers have argued, time is not something we are *in*; it is a mode of our being. Paying taxes (since tenants, not owners, are responsible for property levies), having a bank account, and being employed (if reading and writing what one wants can be called *work*), I was not a visitor; and my inner mode of being as well as outer, on which it was regulated inevitably, if not exclusively, made me a Sheffielder. No matter how abstract, poetry and other emanations of the mind (mathematical matters excepted, perhaps) are a function of the person, and the person is always person-in-the-world. Even—especially—connections with those elsewhere bore, from my end, Royal Mail postmarks, bits of local news, an occasional British locution, and, in unknown quantity, the *weltanschauung* of one whose daily view from the Arts Tower was often of snowdrift hills or twisters of raindrops gyrating just beyond the window, and whose evenings were spent (with many exceptions, of course, when colleagues shared *their* particular time with me) in solitude and silence, pulling my sweater tighter, blocking out through intense denial the ugly antimacassared armchairs and ghastly "art" on the wall, and making, of the British Time—and the time, absolutely—that was allotted to me, a means of consciousness. If, at the moment, a certain chill was cast over things, now the memory of it is a crystal, diamond-hard, a poem whose words, like breath, hang frosted in the air.

Some who love New Mexico, Colorado, and other parts of the West live there already; I must drive all the way through Texas to see them as I wish, seeking higher ground than my Gulf Coast lowlands:

> *Lord, lift me up and let me stand*
> *By faith on heaven's tableland;*
> *A higher plane than I have found,*
> *Lord, plant my feet on higher ground.*

To rise from New Orleans, topographically speaking, is no challenge, since in this city we are below sea level at most points; driving west, I will be on higher ground all the way, ascending more than four thousand feet before leaving Texas. Whether it will be possible to rise in any other sense remains to be seen.

This trip will be different from any I have taken before—including two recorded in these pages—because this is September, the first September I have been free to travel since my academic career began. Said career has recently come to a close; as the Brits put it, I am redundant. No, that is not quite it, since (as readers know) I was not really laid off; a scheme at my university, undergoing its third fiscal crisis of the 1990s, to get rid of some reputedly highly paid senior professors (a few really *were*), certain of whom had been thorns in the administration's side, produced a separation package so attractive that thirty-three faculty members from the Uptown campus, including me, accepted it, thereby decimating two or three departments (but what is that to deans, probably annoyed because they couldn't manage to clear out German also?). I had previously been thinking of this move in order to achieve, in late middle age, the *disponibilité,* or availability, that Gide recommended to the young (practically speaking, possible for only those with an independent income); my decision was facilitated by a university calculation, or miscalculation. So here I am in the last days of summer, soon the early days of fall, in my Jeep Cherokee (bought with such a purpose in mind), crossing Texas toward New Mexico, when I should be standing before the advanced grammar class in Room 308 presenting gender rules (yes, there are numerous such rules in French), reviewing the orthográphic-changing verbs, and drilling the *passé simple* and imperfect subjunctive. Not since October 1949, when in midsemester my father left his job and we pulled up stakes in Colorado to go to Alpine, have I seen in an autumnal light any of the territory I shall soon traverse.

This time, furthermore, my route is different: Houston, as usual; but then Dallas, where, after decades in France, my friend Maggie has just settled; thence in a great hypotenuse along U.S. 287 from Fort Worth to Amarillo. I pass by Bowie, the family seat of a friend—a librarian—and not far from Jacksboro, the birthplace of the eminent critic Lewis P. Simpson, then Archer City, Larry McMurtry's boyhood town. Is there something about these isolated communities on the vast West Texas expanses that made people find life in books? The Archer City house where McMurtry, one of the premier book collectors and antiquarian booksellers in America, now lives and stores *some* of his library belonged at one time to an oilman and rancher, W. H. Taylor, who was himself something of a bibliophile and apparently a great reader. After the accidental death of his son and only child, he gave up his business and sought consolation in books. "The light in his second-floor study burned all night—from my small bedroom in our garage I could look across the hay field and see that light," recalls McMurtry in *Walter Benjamin at the Dairy Queen*. (Part of Taylor's library is now in the house of his wife's nephew, an acquaintance of mine who lives on Royal Street in the Bywater here in New Orleans.)

In Chillicothe (a word meaning, appropriately, "fresh water"), I stop briefly for refreshments. The town is proclaimed as home of a champion bull-rider and the "Fighting Indians." Apparently the busybodies who obliged the Stanford University teams to abandon the offensive ethnic appellation have not found Chillicothe nor, I recall, Red Mesa in Arizona, where the Navajo residents still call their team the Redmen. (These linguistic purges and similar moves initiated by politically correct agitators are mostly divisive, calling attention to what should be only points of departure, not rigid cultural categories, and creating enmity; moreover, they feature and favor the noisiest and least tolerant among the group in whose name they are made, with harmful consequences for some supposed beneficiaries.) Then on past Amarillo to Vega (altitude 4,030), a small town to the west, on the northern edge of the Llano Estacado.

In character, the motel there, located on Route 66 off Interstate 40, is halfway between the standardized variety of the national chains and the old tourist-court type, sometimes called "Mom and Pop." Shutting down the air conditioner, I open the windows to the evening breeze off the High Plains, a wind that plays in a grove of majestic pine trees and heightens the particular twilight feeling in the upper elevations of West Texas—the sense of breath come from afar, the decline in the powerful light, the cooling after day's heat. In the motel restaurant, no alcoholic beverages are available; it may be a dry county, or these folks good Baptists. (Perhaps I should have looked for a package store. But there, I might get the answer I once got in Ozona when I asked the clerk whether she had any chilled wine: "Not any *you'd* want.") For the second evening in a row, having already indulged in Dallas, I order enchiladas—a well-rounded plateful. Other diners come in, including two couples, obviously traveling together, who are driving restored Model-As to some powwow. From the motel room, I have already inspected, surreptitiously, the charming little motorcars of 1930 and 1931 vintage parked near my door: HP 40, beautifully appointed, with stainless-steel trim (according to the owner's boast—I eavesdropped also) and perfect paint. The couples, however, are less well turned out: one man's socks do not match (the left is some four inches higher than the right), and everyone is clad in shorts of a loud pattern or, in one case, purple culottes, and tops that do nothing for the whole effect. One husband says to his wife, "You look tarred." Tarred?—I see no pitch, no feathers. Oh, "tired"—they are Texans. I chat with the server, of Hispanic descent, who informs me, when I tell her it's a nice town, that "you wouldn't think so if you lived here." True, true, at least from her point of view: she is about twenty, and vast skies do not fulfill her dreams.

The next morning begins with the rosy fingers of dawn in the East, but because these are the open plains, the color seems to fill the entire heavenly bowl. Aurora is up late: this is still the central time zone, the same hour as in Pensacola, Florida. I make a quick coffee in the room and munch on a roll Maggie gave me the previous day, then head up the road to Dalhart and Texline, right at the New Mexico line, where a second, more substantial breakfast seems in order. John's Café is just the place: quick service, good food, friendly talk at the counter (but not *too* friendly). Not many days have passed since Princess Diana and her companions were killed in the Pont de l'Alma tunnel, and many have spoken of little else; indeed, the newspapers have informed us that the entire United States is grief-stricken. Yet here at John's, talk doesn't seem to run to the event, nor has mourning laid a pall over the place; *USA Today* must have been mistaken. My arrival does not change things in that respect: I do not rejoice in the accident, but never having identified with her nor sought vicarious thrills in accounts of her activities, I find her death akin to that of a film star or other jet-setter, perhaps even fortunate for her sons. History has been made out of worse. (You may well ask, "Is this the higher moral ground?" Mindful of admonitions that one should not judge, or ask for whom the bell tolls, I do not claim so; at least I shall endeavor to be truthful. Though I recall what Charles Péguy replied, when he was reminded of that evangelical precept: "I don't judge, I condemn.")

The route continues from Texline over the Kiowa National Grasslands to Clayton, New Mexico, and the ranch country of that corner, thence to Raton (elevation 6,640 feet) and Raton Pass, which began as a wagon road laid out by "Uncle Dick" Wootton in 1866, for the use of which he charged $1.50. As Interstate 25 now, it is free. Driving is not free of concern, however; most of the route northward through Colorado is congested. Furthermore, one must go through the hot spots of Trinidad, Walsenburg, and Pueblo before reaching Colorado Springs, my destination for a few days. "Paris is well worth a mass," said Henri of Navarre upon converting to Rome so he could accept the French throne; I do not have to do anything so radical, merely suffer through the traffic and the smelter of Pueblo (4,668 feet) before rising again to more than 6,000 feet at my cousin Beth's house. Jim, her husband, has, like me, recently retired from full-time exercise of his profession, that of engineer. In his newfound leisure, he does a little consulting work, spends more hours with his wife, daughters, sons-in-law, and granddaughters, volunteers at Grace Church and elsewhere, and finds time for a second calling, that of artist. He designs and makes turquoise jewelry, kachina dolls, and other western-style objects; he also paints in oils and other media, and has only to look out his west window to study again the great mountain that Pike sighted as he went north from the Arkansas River, and which Jim has turned into painted (and sometimes profitable) equivalents.

This stop is for visiting, with the living and vigorous and with the dying, as my cousin Frances enters the last week of her life. To hospice visits, we add a restoring day trip over Ute Pass to Woodland Park, then Cripple Creek, in which, along with Central City and Blackhawk, other old mining towns, gambling is now allowed. Every shop and eatery has a row of one-armed bandits, and there are large casinos also, but at least the old nineteenth-century structures remain, the town being a preservation district. In this territory, various kinfolk, including my mother, and kin of kin taught school, built dams, worked as miners, ranchers, and forest rangers; their mark is visible on the land and in my mind.

A few days later, I leave over the same pass (U.S. 24), thence Wilkinson Pass, through which one drops down to the level grasslands of South Park; beyond rises the splendid range of the Collegiates (Princeton, Yale, Harvard, Columbia, Oxford), all more than 14,000 feet high. I turn north on Colorado Route 9 to Fairplay, then over Hoosier Pass (11,541 feet), along the Blue River, to Breckenridge and Silverstone. Those summering and wintering there are mostly snobs; I am a snob. We are, however, at opposite ends of the snobbery spectrum. *They* patronize, and presumably like, the East Coast ice-cream shops and fancy restaurants that have colonized there, along with chic apparel stores and sports shops selling expensive skis and winter regalia. *I* prefer what is authentic and harmonious with a place, a person: native-rock houses in West Texas, log-cabin style in the Rockies, pueblo designs for the desert Southwest, houses built by local people and suitable to the materials and setting. In *Death Comes for the Archbishop,* Willa Cather described this relationship of land and dwelling, as it could be seen 150 years ago: "The Hopi villages that were set upon rock mesas were made to look like the rock on which they sat. . . . The Navajo hogans, among the sand and willows, were made of sand and willows." For Ralph Lauren labels I care not a whit. Unnaturally uniform in shape and coloration, arranged in factitious-looking rows designed obviously by outlanders, the shops in Breckenridge compose a pretentious strip mall about as genuine as a Hollywood set (frequented in fact by some who work on those sets and find meaning there). I had originally thought that Aspen was even worse; readers of this volume now know otherwise.

After Route 9 crosses Interstate 70, mountain simplicity dominates again. My destination is Tabernash, in Grand County and Middle Park, or, rather, Ranch Creek outside of Tabernash, to see my cousin Jean and her husband. The road takes me to Kremmling, a rather tacky railroad and ranching town, then east along U.S. 40 to Hot Sulphur Springs, the county seat, and southward to Tabernash. Much of the route follows the Colorado River (called the Grand within the state of Colorado until the 1920s); part of it winds through Byers Canyon, alongside the Denver & Rio Grande Western tracks. (Going instead along the Front Range—Colorado Springs to Denver—then on Interstate 70 to the U.S. 40 turnoff would have saved time, I believe, but seeing is my game.) Jean has lived in the Fraser Valley since 1951, her husband, Dwight, a bit longer. The altitude is some 8,600 feet. Most nights, even in the summer, the temperature drops below freezing; this past winter, a mild one, it fell no further than 40 degrees below zero, but minus-56 has been registered there. Until recently, their stoves burned only wood. Yet one is comfortable in their place from morning on: windows capture the high mountain sun, and solar cells provide much of the energy needed.

The afternoon I arrive, Dwight, for whom "retire-ment" means a construction business and other enter-prises, has been hauling gravel with his Kenworth eigh-teen-wheeler; Jean returns from a hike with a club, which has involved a rise of 3,000 feet. The club assists with maintenance of the Continental Divide trails. She proposes a similar outing for the next day, but, without boots and surely without practice, I choose something less rigorous, merely a walk around Monarch Lake. This is followed by a visit to the Grand County Historical Museum, of which she has been the moving spirit for years. (Dwight has been a mover, too, and not only in spirit: of the various small buildings that compose the museum complex, only one, an old brick schoolhouse, was originally on the premises, the others having been removed by him from their locations in the environs and transported on his flatbed trailer.) I am taken with the railroad history display, showing how the trans-Colorado route was laid out over Rollins Pass, then, later, through the Moffatt Tunnel. Chiefly, though, I am drawn to an exterior exhibit, the shepherd's wagon, of the sort used by isolated sheepmen in the past, as now. (The following day, en route west, I see two or three wagons up in the sagebrush and a rider nearby, with his dog and scattered sheep.) This one, it is plain, was fitted out to accommodate, as well as possible, all needs, in-cluding lamps for nighttime reading.

Taking leave of Ranch Creek the next day, I head back to Kremmling, then over a gravel county road, angling southwest. This route has been recommended, and with reason. Except for switchbacks on some very steep rises and drops, not for the faint-of-heart, one can make good time, around forty mph, and yet be virtually alone, riding through sage, then forest, and along streams. Pronghorns are visible here and there in the open areas. At State Bridge, one joins a paved road, which leads to Interstate 70; I shall follow it to west of Grand Junction. Although selected by engineers as the most feasible east-west route for interstate traffic in Colorado, and not so rugged as U.S. 50 along the Gunnison further south, it constitutes the most expensive interstate stretch in the nation. Much of it borders the Colorado River, with countless bends and tunnels, and steep descents. Why, along the stretches marked "Speed Limit 50," am I the only one not surpassing that figure? Double-trailer trucks overtake me with a roar, and cars and pickup trucks, following so closely that they seem chained together, *whoosh* past. Do I have a yellow streak? I wish fervently that they would all move out of the way: the scenery is worth more attention from me than it is getting.

Grand Junction and its surrounding area were settled by Mormons. Hardworking, good people in many ways, they do not excel in imagination: they named the north-south roads according to their distance (in miles) from the Utah line, and crossroads by letters of the alphabet. Intermediate roads have such names as 20 3/8 or J 1/2. My cousin Edith and her husband, Bob, having sold their business in Taos, now have some acreage on 21 Road, with a lovely house, backed by a pergola and garden of their design, looking onto Book Cliffs (northward) and (westward) the Colorado National Monument, where Bob is a volunteer ranger once a week. Coming off the interstate, I am a bit confused and turn onto 21 1/2 Road by mistake (not seeing the 1/2 sign). Up and down I cruise, looking for their number, 893. No such; nor can I see anyone who might give me information. Near a white house, with outbuildings, I stop to check the address. No human being appears, but as I turn off the engine, a horse, apparently left without company the whole day long, comes to the fence and neighs at me: the need for society is deep in the equine race, as in the human. I greet him as best I can, not knowing his name. Finally, my mistake becomes apparent to me, so I go a half-mile and there find Edith's.

Our plan is to go camping in Utah. More than once in

the past, my cousins and I did this with sleeping bags and tent, or sometimes no tent. But Edith and Bob, long aficionados of sleeping out, which affords flexibility for exploring and pleasurable time in nature, finally had too much of rains that flooded them and winds that brought to the ground their tent and hanging stew pot: they have bought a fifth wheel. Off we go the next day to Canyonlands National Park and the surrounding area. They are good sports: all this is my idea, and they not only go along to places they have already visited, but Bob (and his dog) pull their fifth wheel behind his pickup, for all of us to cook and sleep in, while Edith keeps me company in my Jeep. Since, even in September, the park campgrounds will be full from noon on, well before we arrive, the only thing to do the first night is pull onto a Bureau of Land Management sagebrush flat; we make a comfortable camp, collecting the breeze at twilight—a sweet essence of the high desert and the La Sal Mountains—and then, after supper, studying the stars.

The next day we undertake, in the Jeep, the main project: going along nearly every paved road, and some dirt ones, that the park, BLM, and state of Utah provide to afford perspectives on the countless canyons of the area, which have been carved out by the waters of the Green and Colorado Rivers. To the motorized visits we will add hikes on foot, since often only by that means can one reach lookout points. One vantage point is offered in Dead Horse Point State Park, a spit of land with a narrow neck where rustled, then abandoned, horses whose escape was cut off by fencing either starved to death or threw themselves into the abyss. The north section of the Canyonlands Park, called "Island in the Sky," provides lengthy drives and several rim overlooks, and we visit them all. The canyons—with strata of red, vermilion, rust, purple, lavender, dark green—ripple in the distance, intersecting one another, creating a labyrinth for the gods. (Indeed, one section of the park is called "The Maze.") Nothing is very close to anything else, and sometimes on the twisting roads one feels hemmed in, almost becalmed in a sea of sagebrush and juniper; yet at any of the innumerable drop-offs, we span vast territory with the eye.

Whereas the mesa tops are generally at right angles to each other, with a smooth, slanting talus at the foot, at Upheaval Dome one has an impressive panorama of nightmarish formations that may be the consequence of a turbulent burst of salt deposits, escaping under pressure, or may have been produced by a striking meteorite. The monstrously irregular shapes are stained by exposed minerals of unearthly hues (uranium among them, mined in the 1960s). Below, at places, one can glimpse the ribbon of river, rickracked in green. I think about John Wesley Powell, the first man (of any race, it is believed)—one armed, at that—who, with a handful of companions, made the canyon journey below, by raft, from the Green River in Wyoming to Grand Wash Cliffs, near what is now Lake Mead. To correlate and synthesize his vision and his views, from far below on the river in 1869, with ours, from these vantage points here on the edge of a canyon and of new century, is impossible in cognitive terms; perhaps only poetry can approximate such understanding.

This exploration is the business of nearly a day. Before sundown, we drive back to the pickup and trailer and head southward, hoping that luck will be with us for a place in Windwhistle Campground, on a BLM road a few miles off U.S. 191. Despite its attractiveness—greater than at the crowded park campgrounds, to my way of thinking—there is plenty of room under the piñon trees, and we make a pleasant camp. The spot is not far from the bottom of a small red sandstone canyon, rather like an amphitheater, with considerable vegetation, even a few ponderosa pines high up in protected pockets. Rock formations of various shapes and smooth daislike mesa tops surround us. At hand are characteristic shrubs and other plants of the region: Gambel's oak, juniper, Mormon tea, Indian rice grass, verbena, sage, Indian paintbrush, chamisa, even yucca. The evening draws on, still bright in the blue above, shadowy beneath the trees, glowing yellow to the west. Blue-gray clouds gather over a mesa rim and darken; rain must be falling somewhere. Then a rainbow forms, soon leaping from one mesa top to another, the entire spectrum showing; it is doubled on one side. All the colors that we saw earlier in the layered canyon walls and the sloping piles of rock below now reappear, glimmering and ethereal, in the strata of heavenly light. Rain falls on us also, and, during the night, come more rain and turbulent winds.

After breakfast the next morning, new drives are planned. One goes past Hatch Point to a BLM overlook, Anticline, which provides a vast panorama. Another takes us to Needles Overlook, which affords a vista over the middle and southern sections of the canyon complex. Some of the afternoon remains, but as it is too late to undertake the roads in the park's southern sector, we head back to Windwhistle for relaxation. The evening will not be so lovely as the previous one, but a bit of rainbow shows again, like a coda or a last musical phrase before the symphony ends.

The following morning, we leave the campground and drive both vehicles to a spot on U.S. 191 where the pickup and trailer can be left for a few hours, then take the Jeep into the southern sector of the park. From the main highway, this is a long but very lovely drive over sagebrush desert, then through a wooded canyon with private ranches, past Newspaper Rock, and at last to a visitor center. The weather is not good—as the Chisholm Trail song puts it, "It's a-cloudin' in the West and lookin' like rain." Rain does indeed fall. But we take in the paved drives and then go down the twisting gravel road to Elephant Hill. A so-called "Jeep trail" that leads off from it is, in my view, not fit for any vehicle, unless you want to ruin your brakes on purpose and then play

Canyonland's version of Russian roulette. We retrace our steps through a mixture of rain and sun that makes the cottonwoods in the river bottom sparkle but augurs ill for the rest of the day.

Rejoining the highway, we retrieve the trailer and set out to Hovenweep National Monument—the Utah portion of this scattered Anasazi site, that is—which has captured my fancy, without my having seen it, and about which I read, then wrote, through cold days last winter. First, we drive down U.S. 191 to Monticello, where we must stop for gasoline in both vehicles, stamps for postcards to friends and family, and a replenishment of supplies at the small supermarket. After the narrow canyon drive and the gravel descent to Elephant Hill, the national highway, paved and shouldered, seems strange—like a pause after heavy exertion. A letup in the rain accommodates us, but shortly it begins again. As we leave the highway and, with the Abajo Mountains behind us, take a side road east toward Hovenweep, misgivings arise in my heart: we have lost time in the storm, and the afternoon grows long in the tooth, or the shadows, during their rare appearance. As we get further into the monochrome wilds, the skies darken and great washes of water attack us from all sides.

Later, pavement gives way to dirt, or, rather, mud, just at the point where we must climb steeply, along a precarious track. I pull over, nerves a bit frayed, and consult with Bob. "Should we go on?" I inquire. Might as well ask that on the high seas; having come thus far, we must proceed still farther: what few towns there are lie miles and miles behind us, over roads now washed out. Bob leads the way, pulling the trailer through the mire (the scene would make a good commercial for Ford trucks); Edith and I grit our teeth and follow, slipping and sliding, despite low gear, grinding slowly upward, then reaching the mesa top, only to find that the road edge has dissolved (visually and materially); we are driving without horizon in undifferentiated gray, buffeted by winds and rain. (El Niño may be to blame, or a Pacific hurricane off the Mexican coast.) Where am I—in the Four Corners or on the Gulf Coast? Since spending the night in the flooded sagebrush is out of the question, we hope that Hovenweep campground will have an open campsite. Miles of utterly desolate landscape surround us, with an occasional Indian reservation road. Finally, we see a small sign indicating "Hovenweep." Blessedly, several sites are available. After the black storm blows itself out, daylight, or rather twilight, reveals a landscaped site, mostly sage, juniper, and piñon, over which presides a huge sky with another rainbow. There is no time for visiting ruins now; that must wait. Dinner seems more welcome than ever: nothing like a pommeling rain and the fear of being stuck in the mire for the night and soaked to the socks to give one an appetite. Edith and I pour a stiff Jim Beam before tackling the steaks she has prepared.

The next morning, the skies are uncertain; one has the feeling that the day will be a washout. In fact, that does not happen; El Niño is indulgent. A long drive awaits us, since we must reach Santa Fe or thereabouts by dark. But some of the morning will be devoted to hiking along footpaths to see the Square Tower and other sections of Hovenweep (a Ute word meaning "deserted valley") accessible from here. I am not disappointed. Then on to Cortez, in Colorado, and Shiprock, New Mexico, near that majestic and sacred landmark of the Four Corners, always thrilling to see, whence we turn east on U.S. 64. The most northerly crossing of the state, taking us into the high Sangre de Cristo Mountains, it affords splendid ascents. We eat lunch by the roadside before continuing our route east, then south. Separation is at hand: at Abiquiu, a lake and campground, we say good-bye, Edith and Bob stopping there for the night, I continuing into Santa Fe so that on the following morning I may make haste to Albuquerque, where I am to give a lecture at the University of New Mexico.

Afterward, New Mexico is not through with me; I have determined to visit on this trip the extreme southwest corner of the state, centered around Silver City, and see its fine forests and the Gila National Monument, which includes cliff dwellings of the Mogollon Indians. First, I must drive south on Interstate 25 for a while, along that messy corridor of modular housing, sprawling roadside businesses, and casino billboards (each pueblo, and they are numerous, has its casino as well as a shop selling curios and the pueblo's distinctive wares). Now that Edith is no longer riding with me, my only company is musical; I put on a Bach and Corelli tape, then Schubert's *Trout Quintet*. The creation of someone who certainly had never visited New Mexican mountains, the latter seems nevertheless peculiarly fitting to my journey, a brilliant correlative of the natural beauty and high spirits of setting and observer. At Socorro, I take, on impulse, U.S. 60 west to Magdalena; this roundabout and mostly solitary route to Silver City will require twice as long as the obvious one but affords extensive acquaintance with what could pass for Longfellow's "forest primeval," pristinely beautiful, with "murmuring pine," spruce, and fir.

Similarly, the next day is spent in the woods—the Gila National Forest and its adjacent protected wilderness—as I drive State Road 15 north to the monument. On the map, it looks like a short hop; signs warn one that it takes two hours. (This is unduly conservative, even for me; my time is something less, and that includes slowing to five mph for bent hairpin curves on a shelf road.) The great tourist mobs do not come up this way. Wildlife benefits from this fact: I see several deer, and twice young ones who have not yet grown into their ears appear just ahead. (One looks at me searchingly.) I cross the Continental Divide for the fifth and sixth times this month. At the monument, one may hike a mile or so to the cliff houses and actually walk among them, inspecting the design of rooms and doors and the ceilings blackened by a generation's worth of winter fires, before the Mogollon went elsewhere, perhaps joining their tradition of square ceremonial rooms to the round kiva tradition of the Anasazi. For the return journey, I follow N.M. 15, the only road out, until it joins another state road angling southeast, and take the latter, to enjoy mountain meadows and canyons, pearlized on this day by rain and mist.

Unfortunately, the third side of the triangle, which I am obliged to follow back to Silver City, runs along a Phelps-Dodge open-pit copper mine. (Just about now I need a caffeine fix; at a crossroads, called a town, there are several cafés and bars, little else. But I deem it unwise to stop; the union types in pickups parked there might not understand that a woman alone, from out of state, could really be on the roads for purposes intellectual, aesthetic, and spiritual.) All the questions of use and misuse of natural resources for the needs and desires of billions of human beings arise when one sees, first the artificial elevations surrounding the pit, dikes as it were, then the inside of the huge, gaping pit itself, the earth inside exposed obscenely. The excavation is inherently ugly; no contour here is natural, and the symmetry and evenness of the graded sides and the interior scrapings and disembowelings do nothing to compensate for the sense that the earth has been violated. Natural barrenness in the desert or even alkali flats are one thing; the ghastly barrenness of a man-made hole where nothing remains but raked mineral substance, is another. What corporations call land restoration will have to be vast and radical to remedy this if the mine is ever deemed unworthy of further exploitation. And maybe by then the corporation will have filed for bankruptcy, so that the people of New Mexico will have to underwrite the reclamation of the land or live with it as it is. Yet do we not want our industries—our alloys, our various tubes and pipes in coolers and heaters, medical equipment, and so on? Perhaps there is some copper coiling in my Jeep or in the space shuttle. To ask these questions is not to answer them; still, better to ask than not.

The next day, I leave Silver City and head toward Texas, via Deming, Las Cruces, and then El Paso. I remember being here as a high-school girl in January 1950, for the Sun Bowl game, at which the Alpine high-school band played. I returned often, including the weeks in 1957 when my mother underwent treatment at a hospital. But my first visit took place when I was about eight, when Mother and I stayed in a railroad hotel (the Fred Harvey) as we stopped over en route to Arizona to join my father, who had gone there for the winter, seeking relief from his ill health and despair. During a moment when Mother went downstairs to see about tickets, I walked through the corridor in my sleep, the uprooting and strangeness of the journey having proven too much for me; she came upon me wandering in the hall. Since then, many other separations have taken place, and there have been partings and farewells that turned out to be eternal; but surely nothing has been more authentic and more existential than the panicked search for the missing parents, the young sense of abandonment portending the separation of each subject and its ultimate, irrevocable solitude.

El Paso, at 3,762 feet, constitutes quite a drop from the elevations I have enjoyed for more than two weeks; except for one last ascent into the Davis Mountains, the high ground of this journey is behind me. Can I discern, in any fashion, in myself or others, moral and spiritual ascent, as well as geographic? Rarely in culture or personal morality is such progress unmistakable. At best, our souls are like cryptogamic soils, where organic growth is minute, slow, easily reversed, but whose progress is necessary if the whole of culture is to prosper. While I cannot make an ethical argument for the wide-open freedom without responsibility that has become the late-twentieth-century version of America's birthright, *perhaps* the human world has improved, if not in this fortnight, at least in my lifetime. The lamps of Europe, which went out in 1914, as Sir Edward Grey said, and would not be illuminated again for long years, have been relit in the last decades of the twentieth century (though plenty of darkness has settled over spots such as Yugoslavia, Algeria, and the heart of Africa, once again a dark continent), and above the cacophonous seductiveness of films, popular music, and television, some notes of a superior culture can still be heard. There are strange hybrids, too, where good and ill keep company: New Mexico is now funding university scholarships through a lottery. As for myself, from the high road and in the intense western light I can look on the human comedy—if not its great evils—with a benign indifference, sometimes even with charity toward my fellows. (I do not forget, however, the maxim I quoted earlier: "He who at age forty is not a misanthrope has never loved mankind.") At closer hand, though, others' foibles may become irritants and break through the skin. Philosophers need a cell or the ivory tower; saints alone carry their beliefs into the street.

Leaving El Paso, Interstate 10 follows the Rio Grande downriver, southeast, then turns directly east; U.S. 90 peels off at Van Horn and dips south to the Big Bend. Of the several homes of my lifetime, this one is closest to my heart, and in some ways I shall not go further or deeper than in contemplation of this desert, where my parents are buried and where a girl I once was is lost too, except for the part that I have managed to preserve or restore. Some salt flats stretch off southward. They aren't much to look at, but animals need the white crystals, and salt has been soldiers' pay. Clumps of salt cedar and greasewood grow there. I think of the biblical salt, the essential, irreplaceable element without which the soul loses its savor. It is as necessary as the waters of renewal, which fill the creeks or rush off the mesas, while enormous, if semidormant, root systems draw in what they can before the spring melt or summer rains are over. Like these roots, I have pumped in broad vistas and moments of high drama when the sun and clouds faced off in tempestuous rivalry above the skyline, or, instead, the mesa displayed for us a panoply of greens, the scarf of Iris, or serene Olympian light. The long way back to New Orleans and the rest of a life are not too much time for replaying it all.